The Religious Right and Christian Faith

BY
GABRIEL FACKRE

WILLIAM B. EERDMANS PUBLISHING COMPANY
GRAND RAPIDS, MICHIGAN

Library of Congress Cataloging in Publication Data

Fackre, Gabriel J.
The Religious Right and Christian faith.

1. Theology, Doctrinal—United States—History—20th century.
2. Fundamentalism—History—20th century. 3. Christianity and
politics—History—20th century. 4. Falwell, Jerry. 5. Moral Majority,
Inc. I. Title.
BT30.U6F33   230'.044   82-2488
ISBN 0-8028-3566-X   AACR2

The author and publisher wish to thank Judson Press for permission
to use material taken from *Youth Ministry* by Jan Chartier and
Gabriel Fackre (Philadelphia: Judson Press, 1979), pp. 11-23, which
appears in revised form in Chapter Two.

To Ben Gabriel Jenkins
a child of the Promise

Contents

Introduction

The Reverend Jerry Falwell has an agenda for the 1980s, "a decade of destiny."[1] Millions of people on the mailing lists of Moral Majority, Inc., share those plans. Together with a wider constituency within the "video church" and similar movements, they seek to register Christian voters, alter science textbooks in public schools, oppose ratification of the Equal Rights Amendment to the U.S. Constitution and liberalized access to abortion, support the development of nuclear power and the restoration of capital punishment, and map events in the contemporary Middle East against an apocalyptic reading of biblical prophecies.[2] These are the people who constitute the formidable new phenomenon of the Religious Right.

Most outside evaluation of this force in American life has come from political and cultural opponents or from those whose interests are sociological and psychological. Mainline churches and mainline evangelicals have just begun to make their assessment.[3] Since the Religious Right is composed essentially of Christian believers, who link their views on contemporary issues to the gospel of Jesus Christ, their brothers and sisters in Christ owe them a response at the level of faith itself. Basic theological assumptions underlie the Religious Right's political positions. These fundamentals need to be examined from a theological point of view. That is what is attempted in this book.

A study of the ethical and political judgments of the Religious Right discloses both explicit and implicit doctrinal views on the nature of God, the state of human nature, the meaning of incarnation and atonement, the purpose of the church, and strong convictions about personal salvation in this world and the world to come. In the following chapters, we shall show how these premises lie behind the literature and political positions of the Religious Right and judge whether they cohere with classical Christian teaching or represent significant departures from it. When such critical scrutiny of vigorous religious movements with political intentions—on the left or the right—has been lacking, the church's mission has always been weakened, accommodation to the culture has been hastened, and in some cases great disaster has ensued.

Responsible evaluation of the Religious Right will strive to give both credit and debit where they are due. Though they might express it more moderately, many critics of the Religious Right would endorse Jerry Falwell's testimony: "I cannot keep silent about the sins that are destroying the moral fiber of our nation. As a minister of the Gospel, I have seen the grim statistics on divorce, broken homes, abortion, juvenile delinquency, promiscuity, and drug addiction."[4] The state of personal morality in the United States *is* deplorable, and the church's silence in the face of it is cause for much soul-searching.

Yet the state of public or social morality demands an equally forthright word from the church. The grim statistics of unemployment among black young adults, the marginal existence of many of society's elders, the danger of a nuclear holocaust because of an unremitting arms build-up, the malnutrition and hunger across the globe, the pockets of poverty in the United States and the cultures of poverty around the world, the destruction of the environment by what we have done or left undone—all these are also there for the minister of the gospel to confront. The "moral scorecard" of the Religious Right reveals blind spots as well.

But if American society has not heard a forceful Christian word about the private virtues from mainline churches, it ill becomes us to judge the Moral Majority for breaking that silence. We ought rather to confess our own sins of omission. After that, however, the critique must come. This critique will have to do with how the Religious Right has made its witness in one area and remained silent in major portions of another.

The assessment in this book, though, seeks to probe beneath the level of moral combat and political encounter to the substructure of theological belief. The styles and strategies of the Religious Right grow out of doctrinal convictions, ways of looking at life and death, God, humanity, and nature. These assertions we shall be testing against long-standing norms of Scripture and Christian tradition.

In documenting the positions of the Religious Right, explicit and implicit, I have made extensive use of the statements and writings of Jerry Falwell. This choice is made for several reasons. As a highly visible and vocal exemplar of the movement we are seeking to assess, Falwell has become a familiar symbol of the new "fundamentalist phenomenon."[5] While differing in some respects from other leaders and constituencies of the Religious Right—on the charismatic issue for example[6]—his views, strategies, and tactics are for the most part representative. Following the trail of his thought through the open plains of carefully prepared press releases and public statements of Moral Majority, Inc., to the narrow and less traveled paths of theology and policy in his writing, preaching, interview responses, and "ecumenical"[7] alliances makes the direction of the Religious Right clearer. For example, Falwell is quite correct to protest against the charge that the political witness of the Religious Right transgresses the church-state boundary. The doctrine of the separation of church and state does not prevent any person or organization, secular or religious, from making opinions known in the public sector. Falwell has learned this lesson well—as he himself testifies—from "the public church"[8] of the 1960s and 1970s as it sought the political implementation of its moral visions. But a careful reading of how the Religious Right is making a political witness and of the specifics of that witness does raise fundamental questions about Falwell's approach which are not answered by simple counterattacks against "the liberals."

The Religious Right, including Jerry Falwell, is much more than Moral Majority, Inc. The stated goals of that latter group sound much like the agenda of many political and religious conservatives—and of some people who would not wish to be identified as such but worry about the tattered moral fabric of the U.S. But reading these moral texts against their larger theological and religious context gives them a meaning that is not apparent on surface scrutiny. The part must be viewed in the light of the whole. That is the intent of this book: to uncover the wider setting of the political positions of Falwell in particular and the Religious Right in general.

Attention to the theological foundations of this contemporary cultural and political movement grows out of my long-range work in doctrinal clarification. My struggle to express the meaning of the person and work of Christ in conversation with contemporary evangelical, liberation, and neo-Catholic options and classical positions has forcefully brought home to me the importance of theological presuppositions. Thus the digging I am currently doing in Christology, as well as my earlier work in systematic theology for the volume *The Christian Story*, informs this inquiry. In analyzing the doctrinal substructure of the Religious Right, I have thus chosen to follow the course of the Christian narrative as set forth in *The Christian Story:* creation, fall, covenant, Christ, church, salvation, and consummation, with an epilogue treating the doctrine of God which emerges from this saga of redemption.[9]

This examination of the conceptual underpinnings of the Religious Right has led me to some conclusions I did not foresee at the outset. Some of these may puzzle or anger both supporters and opponents of the Religious Right at one point or another. I shall argue that in each doctrinal area there are undoubted convergences of the Religious Right with what may be called classical Christian faith. Moreover, there is clear evidence in those same areas of the foe against which the Religious Right has unleashed its bitterest attacks, "secular humanism." In making this charge I define "secular humanism" in its fundamental theological meaning: an anthropocentrism which makes finite human judgment, derived from secular experience, definitive of ultimate truth, and as such sets humanity in the place of deity.[10] This understanding is basic to a biblically grounded theology, for it is rooted in the primal biblical account of secular humanism, when the self-idolatry of the creature fell prey to the temptation, "You will be like God" (Gen. 3:5), and rejected the claims of the Creator. Secular humanism at its deepest root is the act of human self-elevation and the imperialism of human judgment. This arrogance can express itself in the pieties of Adam as well as the manifestos of the atheist. "Not every one who says to me, 'Lord, Lord,' shall enter the kingdom of heaven, but he who does the will of my Father who is in heaven" (Matt. 7:21).

A project like this assumes that there is such a thing as normative Christian belief, a notion that runs counter to the doctrinal relativism pervasive in parts of the church today. Doctrine does develop, enriched by the ever-new light that breaks from God's Word, a light never fully captured in the formulas scribbled in the darkness of our fallen and finite world. But for all the limitations of sight and formulation, we have to do in Christian faith with a core set of visions and affirmations against which the teaching, preaching, and practice of the church must be measured in each time and place.

The material for these chapters was first presented at a 1981 Andover Newton summer school at the Craigville Conference Center in Massachusetts. I am grateful to the pastors and church leaders at that event whose probing questions and comments helped in the clarification of the ideas presented here. Special thanks go to Gregor Goethals, Joseph O'Donnell, William McLinn, and Francis X. Pirazzini, long-time friend as well as fellow summer faculty member, for their colleagueship. As with all my writing, this book has received the loving critique of my spouse Dorothy and has also been influenced by the thinking and research of my daughter and son-in-law, the Reverends Gabrielle and Gary Jenkins. I am grateful to Gabrielle for compiling the Index. Kay Coughlin, Andover Newton faculty secretary, has done her usual industrious and competent work of typing.

—GABRIEL FACKRE

The Religious Right
and Christian Faith

CHAPTER 1

The Spectrum of Politics and Piety

The best way to identify the constituency of the Religious Right is to place it in relationship to other points of view at the far right end of the political spectrum in America today. The extent to which there is active collusion among these groups, with their allied perspectives, is difficult to discern, especially as one gets to the further reaches of the right-wing continuum. The collegiality of the Religious Right and what students of contemporary American politics call the New Right is evident, for example, throughout a book by New Right political organizer Richard Viguerie, for which Jerry Falwell wrote the introduction. Regardless of uncertainty about deliberate cooperation, however, we may confidently place the Religious Right on a *political* spectrum because it has emerged on the American scene in terms of the political causes it espouses. Yet its institutional forms, motivation, and intellectual framework make it a religious entity; hence the qualifier "*Religious.*" While its institutions and their members are primarily Christian, some Religious Right organizations try to encompass a wider group of American citizens, and almost all of its single-issue campaigns address their appeal beyond Christians. Moral Majority, Inc., for example, seeks to include Jews and Mormons as well as Christians, Roman Catholic and Protestant.[1] Thus the term Religious Right is more appropriate than Christian Right.

The centerpiece of the Religious Right is Moral Majority, Inc., with its founder and leader Jerry Falwell. Falwell began this organization at the urging of a number of New Right figures, especially Richard Viguerie and Paul Weyrich.[2] Moral Majority, Inc., has (according to Falwell) a mailing list of four million people, which is computerized, personalized, and broken down into a variety of demographic categories. It makes its influence felt by publishing broadsides, fostering "Love America" rallies, launching pressure campaigns on single issues, and building up a network of chapters around the country which are given freedom to pursue concerns in their own area and in their own way under the umbrella of the Moral Majority philosophy. Its impact in the several years of its existence has been impressive—in the political arena, in the media (*New Yorker* magazine devoted no less than eighty pages to Falwell and the Moral Majority in May 1981),[3] and in the general North American moral and intellectual climate.

Falwell is also pastor of the 18,000-member Thomas Road Baptist Church in Lynchburg, Virginia, served by a staff of sixty clergy. The congregation has founded a Christian academy, Liberty Baptist College, and an alcoholic rehabilitation clinic. It broadcasts a television program which is aired over 304 stations in the United States and 69 abroad to a listening audience in the neighborhood of one and a half million.[4] Falwell is a prolific speaker and writer. His best-known statement of the Moral Majority philosophy is the book *Listen, America!*[5]

Near the center of the Religious Right, and often pre-eminent in their capacity for spectacular and artful presentation of religious and political themes, are the other politically oriented preachers and programs of the "electronic church." While figures like Pat Robertson of the "700 Club" and Jim Bakker of the "PTL Club" shared in some aspects of an early political-religious coalition—for example, the Religious Roundtable—they subsequently withdrew. Less formally and directly associated with the Moral Majority, they do consistently espouse political causes and perspectives on current events similar to Falwell's, and their theological views are virtually identical.[6] Other television evangelists, like James Robison, have an explicit religio-political involvement in the Falwell tradition. Still others like Rex Humbard, Oral Roberts, and Jimmy Swaggart maintain their own individual slants and points of view and constituencies, but cluster theologically on the right and occasionally draw the implications of this stance for current affairs.

Usually allied with the foregoing, in theological sentiment and political program, are many religiously motivated or supported single-issue groups. They include the newer hard-line pro-life groups, elements of the older pro-life coalitions, anti-homosexuality movements, pro-family groups, and anti – sex education, anti-ERA, pro-prayer in public schools, anti-pornography constituencies. Their activities range from launching nationwide campaigns to prevent ratification of the Equal Rights Amendment to a local Religious Right congregation picketing the Planned Parenthood dinner at a downtown congregation of the United Church of Christ. The theological convictions and political actions characterizing these single-issue groups (and the occasional networks within and among them) mark them as very much a part of the Religious Right.

Another component of the Religious Right is the national religio-political groups that focus on legislation, evaluate elected officials and candidates for office, and seek to influence national policy. The best-known groups are Christian Voice, which rates Members of Congress according to how it judges their support on selected moral issues, and Religious Roundtable, which alerts clergy to issues of moment to the Right and sets forth a point of view on those issues.

As these pieces of the Religious Right fall into place, both its uniqueness and power become apparent. Robert Sandon has pinpointed four factors to account for its novelty and effectiveness:[7] (1) The independence of television evangelists, who need no accountability to larger ecclesial communities; (2) the links between the Religious Right and the political right; (3) a pragmatic "reverse ecumenism," which allows separatist Protestant fundamentalists—who once would have had nothing to do with Roman Catholics, Mormons, and Jews—to work with them on common concerns; (4) the rise of "Christian academies," whose numbers have increased in seventeen years from a handful to 16,000, with a new one appearing every seven hours according to Falwell. These supply a leadership pool to Moral Majority, Inc., and other movements of the Religious Right.

Implicit in Sandon's list are two other factors. One is the use of contemporary techniques to communicate religious and political ideas, not just television and radio broadcasts, but also computerized direct mail, telephone trees, and management techniques. Second is a mainstreaming tendency in the Religious Right, which has moved it from the fringes of American society to the center of the action, though not the center of the spectrum. When the President of the United States places a call to Jerry Falwell in response to his criticism of a Supreme Court nomination, it is obvious that things have changed from the days when radio preacher Carl McIntire's volleys broadcast over more than 500 radio stations were largely ignored by the powers that be.

A second major type of right-wing political philosophy and practice is represented by the professedly secular right. Here very similar moral and political goals are espoused but without a formal religious identification. They may be grouped in proximity to the Religious Right, not only because of similarities in their political and moral sensibilities and alliances and crossover of personnel, but because their intellectual presuppositions do bring them into the theological arena. These secular groups do function with assumptions about the nature and destiny of humankind correlative with, or competitive to, Christian belief. For our purposes here we may draw attention to the figures and movement of the New Right:

—para-political organizers such as Richard Viguerie, Paul Weyrich, Howard Phillips, and Timothy Dolan, and para-political financial resources such as Joseph Coors, Richard Mellon Scaife, and the Hunt brothers.

—para-political organizations such as the Heritage Foundation, the Conservative Caucus, the National Conservative Political Action Committee (NCPAC), the Committee for the Survival of a Free Congress (CSFC).

—political leaders such as Senators Jesse Helms of North Carolina, Paul Laxalt of Nevada, Strom Thurmond of South Carolina, and Orrin Hatch of Utah.

—single-issue movements: pro-nuclear, anti—gun control, pro-military, pro—capital punishment, right-to-work.[8]

A third band on the spectrum of the right, in ambivalent and sometimes hostile relationship to the Religious Right, is the Radical Right. Despite significant differences, the supporters of the Radical Right do promote the cause of the Religious Right, endorse many of its single issues, and share some of its underlying premises about the nature of things. The Radical Right is marked by the acerbity of its attacks on foes, the rigor of its orthodoxy, and the extremism of its views and sometimes of its tactics. But it is not a monolith. We may distinguish between "soft radicals" and the "hard radicals."

—Soft radicals include such long-time warriors as the late William Loeb of the *Manchester* (N.H.) *Union Leader*, former New Hampshire governor Meldrin Thompson, Fred Schwarz, of the Christian anti-Communist Crusade,[9] the John Birch Society, religious radical rightist Billy James Hargis of the Christian Crusade, and the redoubtable Carl McIntire of the 20th-Century Reformation Hour.

—Hard radicals (whose ideology, tactics, and programs explain the adjective) are represented by the Ku Klux Klan and neo-Nazi movements and their local and regional counterparts. Their occasionally caustic comments about Falwell and other Religious Right figures clearly warn against a simplistic identification of the Religious Right with the hard Radical Right.

Having placed the Religious Right along the current political continuum, we must go on to locate it on the religious spectrum, so that the Religious Right is not confused with others who on the surface share its piety. That is the reason for the following breakdown of contemporary evangelicalism, of which the Religious Right is a professed part.

The word evangelical, as Falwell himself has noted,[10] is subject to such variation these days that it no longer conveys a clear meaning. In a broad sense the term refers to the authority of Scripture and the belief in salvation by grace through faith (*sola Scriptura, sola fide*). As expressing the formal and material principles of the Reformation, "evangelical" has been

5

used in the names of various European churches since the 16th century. A narrower meaning of the term has been shaped by piety on the American scene. This sense of "evangelical" includes the traditional features, but with the connotation that they are internalized by a conversion experience and externalized in rigorous moral and spiritual disciplines. Thus "born-again Christianity" has become an important contemporary meaning of "evangelical." That will be our usage in this typology. From right to left:

—*Fundamentalists*: This group is characterized by a "biblical inerrancy" view of the authority of Scripture (belief in the plenary verbal inspiration of the biblical autographs, which has been protected by the grace of preservation over the centuries as the Bible has come to us in selected translations and editions), a separatist relation to other Christian bodies, and a militancy in defending its doctrines against all foes. Fundamentalists may be apocalyptic or nonapocalyptic, political or apolitical. The Religious Right is a subset of fundamentalism, apocalyptic and political.

—*Old Evangelicals*: Here are found the born-again Christians who stress the conversion experience and holiness of life and seek to nourish these in the revival tradition and in congregations of fervent piety. But they do not put a premium on separatist activity or biblicist polemics, nor do they establish strong political allegiances or feature apocalypticism.

—*New Evangelicals*: With at least a thirty-year history in the United States, roughly corresponding to the life of the magazine *Christianity Today*, these evangelicals insist on the ethical and political relevance of faith as articulated by broad guidelines, stress the intellectual viability of a born-again faith and of orthodox theology, and seek to work out their point of view within, as well as alongside of, traditional denominations.

—*Justice and Peace Evangelicals*: Of more recent vintage in the United States, this group is also represented by newly founded periodicals—*The Other Side* and *Sojourners*. These born-again Christians express their faith in more radical political and ecclesial idiom. Whether from an Anabaptist or high Calvinist perspective, they call into question what they see as the accommodation of today's culture and churches to affluence, militarism, and unjust social and economic structures. Many of them seek to embody their faith in an alternative style of life through intentional Christian communities.

—*Charismatic Evangelicals*: Often apolitical (but not necessarily so, especially in the Third World), members of this experiential group within evangelical piety reach out for highly visible signs of the Spirit, primarily the gifts of tongues-speaking (glossolalia) and healing, and intensity of prayer, song, and communal life.

In evangelicalism, as in all dynamic movements, there is mobility among and within the various types. The reality is clearly not as neatly structured as the above catalog suggests. But schemas have their place, and this one is meant to show the connections of the Religious Right with their evangelical brothers and sisters, and also the significant differences between them and other evangelicals.

The identity of the Religious Right is determined by the specific "for and against" campaigns it wages, as well as its site on the political spectrum and the evangelical continuum. With only the slightest variations, the Religious Right maintains a common front with the political New Right.[11]

The typical inclusive term which the Religious Right uses for the values, institutions, programs, policies, and persons that express and embody the power of Satan in our society is "secular humanism." Ironically, for an authoritative definition of this evil, some in the Religious Right cite French Reformed philosopher Jacques Ellul, whose Barthian point of view would itself fall under their censure (and who might well use the very concept to attack the acculturation of the Religious Right—a point we shall explore subsequently).[12] Secular humanism is seen basically as a view of a world without God and thus without any absolute values. Those values denied in principle or in fact are understood as the moral absolutes of the Judeo-Christian tradition.

Violation of sexual norms and the theoretical legitimation of this breakdown come under the severest attack: homosexual practice and its defense as an "alternative life-style"; abortion and its pro-choice ideologues; pre-marital sex, adultery, and divorce; sex education in the public schools—which is believed to encourage sexual promiscuity; feminism and its alleged denial of the hierarchical family order, encouragement of lesbianism and general promiscuity, and destruction of true feminity; governmental endorsement and encouragement of feminist goals; promulgation in the media, especially television and cinema, of all the foregoing; the beat of rock music and the rhythms and habitat of the disco which contribute to the atmosphere of moral degeneracy; the easy availability of modern literature, with its sexual promiscuity and deviancy in public schools and public libraries; the pornographic magazine and book trade which feeds on contemporary prurience; the liberal church's flirtation with situation ethics in its teaching on sexuality; and the general breakdown of family life manifested in and facilitated by all these trends.

Besides promoting immorality, secular humanism is thought to erode our liberties, particularly economic ones. Its zeal for power and its misdirected idealism come together in socialistic experiments and the spreading of government's tentacles over the rights of free citizens. Thus the capitalist economy endorsed by the Scriptures[13] and the God-given prerogative of pursuing profit are shackled. Fulfilling the biblical injunction to have dominion over the earth is hampered by the legislative bondage promoted by secular environmentalists. Similar improper restraints have been placed upon the nuclear industry by the machinations of secular humanism and its socialist stepchild. The public school system displays the pronounced influence of secular humanism on government. Evidence of this is ample, says the Religious Right, in the promulgation of a relativistic value system, especially in the area of sexual morality, in the eviction of God from school premises by the Supreme Court decision about prayer in the public schools, and in the representation of the secular humanist theory of evolution as scientific fact while the "creationist" alternative is denied equal time. Again, government encourages sloth and rewards deviousness through welfare programs. Its plenitude of social services discourages the virtues of initiative and personal responsibility.

While the government, animated by secular humanism, extends its influence into areas where it does not belong, the Religious Right sees it as abandoning the very concerns for which it was designed in domestic affairs: law and order. It coddles criminals instead of punishing them, relaxes necessary measures such as the death penalty, and does not adequately support the police or allow the FBI to do its job. Given the lawlessness of our secular society, the basic right to own and defend one's property is seriously threatened by current proposals for gun control, one more example of a tyrannical government's attempt to destroy the private rights of its citizens. The dangers of government today are reinforced by the technology available to it. Thus the power of the Social Security system, not only to redistribute wealth unfairly but to monitor and control our lives through its classification system and records, constitutes a peril.

Among the Religious Right's sharpest indictments of the U.S. government pertain to its external responsibilities, defense and foreign policy. The permissiveness that marks secular humanism in its views on sexual morality and domestic legislation is seen as carrying over to international affairs. America has gone soft on its greatest enemy Communism and has allowed its military muscle to atrophy. It is fast becoming a weak sister in the family of nations, losing out to Soviet encroachments, giving up the Panama Canal, suffering humiliation in Iran, coddling socialist nations in the Third World, flirting with Communist China, nitpicking with its friends about human rights, thus weakening their effectiveness as allies in the struggle against Communism. A sign of its deteriorating will and of the loss of the original vision of America's special role under God is the erosion of military power represented by years of failure to build up an arsenal of new weapons, particularly those of nuclear capability.

Against the invasion of secular humanism the forces of the Religious Right and its ally the political New Right are poised. Indeed, we "are fighting a holy war," says Falwell.[14] In the area of sexual morality, the following counter-movements and armies are being mobilized: campaigns against homosexual rights legislation, particularly laws which permit avowed homosexuals to teach in public schools; campaigns to outlaw or restrict abortion and to establish it ideologically and legally as murder; efforts to strengthen traditional morality, where possible through laws discouraging pre-marital sex, divorce, and adultery; all-out resistance to feminism as an ideology, including support for anti-ERA and anti—woman draft movements; campaigns against contemporary rock music; concerted efforts to remove from libraries and public schools books considered to be undermining moral values; full-scale war against pornography, including the monitoring and evaluation of television programs and the boycott of products sold by those who sponsor disapproved programs; articulation of a "Total Woman" philosophy as an alternative to feminism; training in the ways of hierarchial family life, which entail the obedience of wives to husbands, strict discipline for children, and family-centered roles for the wife and mother. Where possible, the Religious Right's campaign against the sexual immorality of secular humanism presses for governmental changes. There is a demand for the removal of sex education from public schools, campaigns against all kinds of drugs including alcohol, the effort to make pornography illegal, campaigns against ERA and for abortion legislation, and a drive for a comprehensive family bill which will, as far as possible, embody in law the moral standards represented by the Religious Right.

In the domestic affairs of the nation beyond sexual morality, the Religious Right supports and organizes programs to controvert secular humanism in present or proposed policies and seeks to establish its own agenda. Thus it organizes for removal of or resistance to any government restraints on making a profit, exploiting natural resources, using weapons, police power, executing criminals. It seeks to eliminate government support for the extension of the rights of women, government protection of organized labor, and government programs to aid marginal citizens considered by the Religious Right strong enough to do without this aid and perverse enough to exploit it. These various efforts are embodied in national mobilizations. Furthermore, the effort to challenge the secular humanism of public schools is embodied in the formation of Christian Academies, an alternative educational system, in the re-introduction of prayer in the public schools, and in the insertion of a creationist view of the origins of the world along with the evolutionist view.

In international affairs the Religious Right is a consistent supporter of arms development, particularly nuclear weaponry, and the dissemination of armaments among U.S. allies; of friendship with countries having right-wing political leadership and the diminution of concern about human rights issues in such nations with right-wing dictatorships; of extensive enlargement of the military budget and the build-up of armed forces; and of a militant posture toward the USSR and other Communist and socialist countries. The Religious Right is a regular critic of the United Nations and a proponent of its diminished significance. And because of the specifics of its eschatology, which we shall examine subsequently, it is an unswerving supporter of the state of Israel.

Running through all the political views and actions of the Religious Right is a sharp attack on mainstream churches, which it sees as accommodating to the philosophy of secular humanism and as a result providing knee-jerk support for many of its rival political positions. "The liberal churches are not only the enemy of God but the enemy of the nation."[15]

The issues and positions of the Religious Right are distinguished from earlier right-wing political movements and traditional conservative political efforts in two important respects. First, the Religious Right draws the lines of political controversy in Armageddon-like terms. This is a holy war which spares no rhetoric and leaves no room for compromise. The theological warrants for this will become clearer when we examine the underlying doctrine of the Religious Right more carefully. Second, the Religious Right makes use of sophisticated modern technology: extensive and skilled use of television, telephone networks, computerized mailing systems, and the latest forms of organizational development. The mustering of legions of supporters and their astute deployment for political action can be traced to the success of these special methods. Of course other factors contribute significantly: the psychology of the times, the sociology of the constituency involved, the political climate of our era, and, of major consequence, the focus of this book—the theological underpinning.

Before we go into this fundamental faith stance, we should look at one last feature which situates the Religious Right, the immediate historical context of its birth and growth.

CHAPTER 2

The Historical Setting
of the Religious Right

The Religious Right has a long ancestry. The church historian
can trace its lineage to the Reformation in both its magisterial
and left-wing expressions. Calvin's Geneva can be seen as a
prototype of efforts to organize society under the moral and
religious rules of a sovereign God. Even more, various elements
of Anabaptist piety live again in today's Religious Right: a church
life drawn apart from a corrupt culture, an evangelistic zeal,
and a determination to transform the political community into
the kingdom of God, although not by the militarily violent methods of Münzer and Münster.[1]

The American church historian, in particular, will find roots
of the Religious Right closer at hand, in New England Puritan-
ism and also in the apocalypticism in the country's religious
and moral sensibilities and the right-wing eruptions in American political history.[2] Again, historians of religious thought may
well go back further than the Reformation to ferret out connections between today's Religious Right and the long tradition
of Christian dualism which can be traced through the Middle
Ages, to Bardaisan in the second century after Christ and the
Manicheans in the third, and even to Zoroastrianism as it influenced post-exilic Judaism.

Unraveling such historical interrelationships is a special-
ized study to which we can make only passing reference here.[3]
More pertinent to our inquiry are some recent developments
that set the stage for the posture and activity of the Religious

Right today. Over the years I have devised a visual typology for interpreting the changes and direction of contemporary social movements. Here I have developed it as a way of understanding the rise of the Religious Right.[4]

We may begin our look at this more recent historical context with the 1960s. Falwell, an early critic of Martin Luther King, Jr., and civil rights activists (see his sermon "Ministers and Marchers"), has done an acknowledged about-face on the validity of church involvement in civil affairs.[5] Furthermore, the visionary tendencies of that time, albeit in reverse image, are clearly at work in the Religious Right. Thus we begin with the ferment of that decade, when people "had a dream" and sought to move up out of the "pit" toward the "sun" of peace and freedom. Gibson Winter has identified the issues of that era as "being, having and belonging," the questions of war and peace, poverty and race. Let us follow the journey of change agents of that era.

Invariably those efforts to move up and out of the pit were launched by a strategy of education, conscience training, and consciousness raising. Whether it was the civil rights movement, the peace movement, the ecology effort, or the hunger crusade, the teachers and the preachers had their day. And so we portray our typical 1960s change agent as an exhorter, with tract in hand. Thus we start our figure up the incline.

Moral pedagogy has always been characterized by both strengths and weaknesses. Minds can be changed and hearts moved, but the reformer soon learns that wrongdoing is rooted in systems and structures as well as in the inner recesses of conscience and thought. Thus, our change agent concludes that institutions as well as individuals have to be altered. How is this to be done? The offending patterns and parties must be called before the bar of justice. Visionary movements sought redress of grievances in the courts of law.

We place our figure a little further up the earth wall to signify the advances made and also the intensification of pressure.

The gains that can be made by the appeal to law are well known. The 1954 Supreme Court desegregation ruling was a landmark in American justice. Yet those who experienced this forward step discovered also the resistance that remained. Even the best laws can be frustrated by those who administer them or choose not to do so. Furthermore, bad laws must be replaced by good ones and new legislation must be developed to embody new visions of liberty and justice for all. To overcome these new hurdles, our visionary begins pressing somewhat harder, risking more confrontation, making the move from law to politics. Our escalating figure parts the curtain of the voting booth to throw out the offenders and put in responsible persons.

The effort to secure rights for the aggrieved through political action made significant strides in the 1960s and continues to do so. But visionaries dreamed of better things and faster progress. The conscience of America had to be stung more aggressively. The invisible poor and oppressed had to be given much higher visibility. And so those who sought change moved out of the voting booth and into the streets. It was time to march!

Where economic power could be wielded, the boycott and strike were joined to the street demonstration. These moves to give a higher profile to injustice were carried out with scrupulous attention to law and order. The constitutional right of public assembly to air grievances was attested with a permit from City Hall. The upward climb is now represented by the picket sign.

With the aid of the media, particularly televised reports of civil rights marches and demonstrations, the attention of the country at large was riveted on the manifest evidences of discrimination and injustice. The growing sympathy for the maltreated showed itself in the withering of longtime discriminatory practices in public accommodations, voting rights, and education.

But change also evoked resistance. Furthermore, institutional racism seemed as intractable as ever in such areas as housing and jobs. Visionaries, in both frustration and hope, moved one crucial step beyond legal protest. The time had come for self-conscious acts of civil disobedience. The individual is accountable to a higher law, which takes precedence over the laws of the state. At first most activists maintained that one must carry on the necessary acts of civil disobedience in a nonviolent fashion. One must be ready to face the consequences—usually imprisonment. Our visionary figure "goes limp," prepared for a trip in the arms of the law.

The sight of respectable citizens being ushered into police vans, faithfully recorded on the evening TV news and in the morning paper, had an effect. Eyes widened and tempers flared,

especially when it was a prominent minister or fully habited nun being incarcerated, but the effort to change unjust social patterns was unquestionably serious. Consciences were being touched and more significant advances were made.

But it was not enough. Unmoved and seemingly untouched by all these strategies were the poor who crowded into the festering inner-city slums. Being able to sit in the front of the bus or to go to college or to move to suburbia or to get a job with IBM was all well and good for middle-class blacks formerly denied access to these experiences. But things looked very different to those who were unsure where the next meal was coming from, living in the squalor tolerated by the slumlord, lacking skills for a job, daily confronting junkies and pushers on one's front stoop. If someone does not turn down the heat under such a pressure cooker, there is bound to be an explosion.

In the middle 1960s the inner cities of America erupted. Frustration targeted the symbols of the establishment closest at hand, the ghetto merchants, but the rage of many days soon spilled beyond them to any object that represented the world of the privileged. That world was within reach and waiting to be "ripped off." In the language of the ethicist, this unpremeditated outrage and plunder is "random violence." Those struggling out of the abyss seized the closest weapon at hand, the rock ready to be hurled at the plate glass window.

How much "progress" was in fact made by this explosion of the urban centers is still much debated. Certainly the riots left no doubt that the layer of civility covering the boiling resentment of an American underclass was thin indeed. The fears generated in "middle Americans" by the havoc wreaked in these outbreaks hardened the resistance of many. A growing polarization grew in American society between those seeking change and those digging in to keep things the way they were.

In the midst of this estrangement and ferment, new cries began to emerge from those seeking redress of grievances. "Power" was the premise and the slogan. Social, economic, and political power continued to be sought, but a more ominous note was also struck as pictures of enraged revolutionaries with rifles in hand appeared in the underground press. Militants were learning the martial arts and arming themselves, speaking of the need to defend their turf. But it was not all defense. There were also calls for—and sometimes execution of—forays into the world beyond, now unambiguously identified as enemy territory. Dissenters against the war in Vietnam followed roughly the same steps up the mountainside as those in the human rights struggle as they came abreast of the freedom revolution in the late 1960s.

About the same time a movement from random violence to "instrumental violence" could be discerned. Planned assaults replaced the earlier pressure-cooker blow-ups. The assumptions of reformers who thought change could be effected within the limits of conventional social protest were consciously rejected. Since society was not going to move further, the time had come for more dramatic tactics.

The process followed a course something like this. First, planned violence was directed toward property—thus the torch in the hands of the revolutionary in our diagram to symbolize the arson of the ROTC building on campus or the firebomb in the downtown bank. Warnings were given beforehand to avoid endangering life, for these activists still sought to contain the violence to property. But that limit did not last long. The establishment's stiffening resistance and seeming imperviousness to this strategy produced further rage and with it assault on persons as well as property. Its early stages included talk of kid-napping and some actual incidents of it, focusing on symbols of corporate power as the victims. Next came the rhetoric of assassination, and some outright murders of people thought to be key representatives of the enemy. Finally, in theory and in scattered practice came guerrilla warfare, conducted in hit-and-run fashion against centers and symbols of corporate power.

The polarization that had begun earlier now deepened profoundly. The total challenge to the institutions of society on the part of the handful who sought to push the movement up and out by one violent leap met with intense resistance from nearly every section of society. And this last desperate charge seemed to exhaust those who attempted it. The surge of change appeared to come to a grinding halt. The agents of change were in disarray, and the visionaries themselves seemed to abandon their efforts and, in fact, to tumble back down into the pit.

About the beginning of the 1970s, when great visions of achievement were everywhere collapsing, some new signs of ascent were beginning to be seen. But this quest for freedom and peace took a very different direction. The movement up and out took place on another side of the pit. Turning their backs on the effort to change conditions, people chose to leave the institutions rather than alter them. The first step in this direction was the departure that we shall identify as "tripping out"—withdrawal from the oppressive society. Some of those wearied by the civil rights struggle in the U.S. talked of returning to Africa. Others sought to repossess the African heritage by withdrawing into the world of black pride and black identity in their own communities. Neighborhoods, new cities, and even the creation of a state within the United States were among the possibilities mentioned for creating "liberation turf." A parallel to this in the war protest effort was the flight of draft resisters to Canada or Sweden.

"Tripping out" had a very different connotation for other frustrated visionaries. In the drug subculture the term referred to the chemical inducement of ecstasy. By soft or hard drugs, the individual sought to create within his or her own psychic world the freedom and peace denied in the institutional area. "Turning on" really meant turning inward and away from the perils and frustrations of the social order. If the right ingredients were inhaled or swallowed or injected, one could think it possible to see the light, even deep in the pit.

While some sought to trip up and out, others, perhaps disillusioned with the claims of physical or psychical escape, began the quest for freedom and peace by forming a counter-community on the edges of the oppressive world. In the intense group experience among those who shared the same pilgrimage, something of the peace and freedom denied by the world might be tasted. "Getting together" became the slogan. Rural and urban communes represented full-scale attempts to provide an alternate way of economic, political, and social living. Others sought the benefits of getting together in psychodynamic form through the weekend human potential experience or the year-long therapy group. Here was an opportunity to "let it all hang out": the broken dreams on the one hand, and the hunger for liberation and reconciliation on the other.

The quest for heaven on earth by way of communitarian experiment or therapeutic group life led many to the conclusion expressed in Sartre's play *No Exit* that hell is other people. Too sanguine a confidence in the possibilities of a colony of light was shattered by the discovery of the shadow side in human relationships. Groupness, as such, did not seem to be able to bring salvation. Something more was needed. For a number of those seeking the light, disillusionment with togetherness prompted a turn in and down. Meditation and contemplation, with the aid of wisdom from the East, would put one in touch with the vision. Exercises and illuminations were imported from the religions of the Far East, and many flirted with the paper-

back thoughts and cults of the latest guru or swami. Neomysticism was in.

Many social historians doubt that American culture, activist and pragmatic and shaped by the Judeo-Christian tradition, can provide firm rootage for exotic Oriental religions. So it seemed in the 1970s as the interest in faddish neomysticisms declined. But the religious quest itself in fact accelerated, though taking a very different direction—not in and down but out and up. The new pietisms of the 1970s appeared, signaled by the characteristic sign of the Jesus People: a finger pointing upward to heaven where Christ reigned and from whence he would soon come again. From the early "Jesus freak" movement to its more sedate Jesus People phase, through the charismatic ferment to "born-again Christianity," the revival fires burned. Like its forerunners on this side of the chasm, our figure did not see the task as one of changing oppressive social and economic systems. Rather, individual conversion was the focus. Indeed, the individual might in turn take responsibility for changing social and economic circumstances, but more often than not the religious task was to prepare for the apocalypse to come.

While multitudes in the 1970s became citizens of the evangelical empire, countless others still inhabited the secular city. The thirst of many of these this-worldly people for mystery and meaning was quenched by intra-mundane unknowns. From the pages of the *National Enquirer* to the tales told by a random university scientist, there was talk of extraterrestrial mystery. Thus, our quester now looks up and out for UFOs. From *Star*

Wars and "Star Trek" to *Close Encounters of the Third Kind*, those who reached for something more were lured beyond. And that beyond may also include other ranges of the unknown, perhaps from the depths of *Jaws*, Atlantis, and the Bermuda Triangle to the lengths of science fiction events yet to come.

Not everyone was able to stretch toward either a religious empyrean or the secular stars. In the 1970s more conventional unrest with things as they are sometimes took form as a grasp for the past. Meaning in the shadowed world of the present was sought in the search for roots. Mooring is to be found in traditions and beginnings—in the way we were, not in the way we shall be. In nostalgia for older values—political, social, personal, economic—or in the traditions of our forebears or ethnicity or lineage we can find our identity. Hence the reach backward, the grasp for firm roots.

Today there are some representatives of all of the foregoing urges and surges, but a new tendency is gaining increasing visibility as well. Repeated attempts to scale the heights, with all the attendant frustrations, have taken a toll among many questers. Is there a way out? Many are answering that question in the negative. They conclude that efforts to change from outside or inside are futile; so why bother? Let's be content with our plight. Let's stop struggling to clamber out of the pit; let's just settle in and make ourselves as comfortable as possible. Look out for yourself—after all, no one else is going to.

Therefore, for some it is now time to dig in. Our pilgrim hollows out a cave in the pit's side, removed from the struggles, and seeks to make himself or herself as comfortable as possible. One attends to one's own needs—hence it is a cave of mirrors where narcissism can be given full play. To insulate ourselves from the cries of need on the other side of the pit and the groans of those climbing up our own side, we put on stereophonic earphones and stare at our TV sets. Surrounded by shiny new technology, we settle into self-indulgence to make the best of a hopeless situation. And because the vision never entirely leaves alone even such a creature, one spins out a "selfist" theory to justify this flight from responsibility.

Just as the rock at the top closed off the efforts of the pilgrims on one side, so the cave signals the end of this line. What future is there for a "me generation" retreating into its subterranean womb? Social commentators such as Aleksandr Solzhenitsyn lash out at this soft, self-centered culture.

At the very time when the escapism of the apolitical center, and the fragmentation of the political left seemed to be leading nowhere, momentum was gathering on the right. Early indicators of it were seen in the evangelical impulses of the 1970s, and one might argue that it also drew on the orientation to the past and communal tendencies of that period. It shared in its own way those other movements' sense of the perilous state of the nation and their dream of lifting it out of its darkness to freedom and peace. The triggering events and perceptions of evil, as well as the diagnosis and prescription, were indeed very different.

Jerry Falwell's own explanation of the formation of the Moral Majority is representative of the analysis of the Religious Right. He lists four factors: the pornography explosion; intervention by the Internal Revenue Service in the operation of private Christian schools; the fairness doctrine of the Federal Communications Commission and its application to the rights of homosexuals to respond to criticism; the abortion ruling by the Supreme Court.[6] Sometimes the 1962 ruling of the court on school prayer is also mentioned as a catalyst. All of these involve government action; all are symptoms of social decay by the diagnosis of the Religious Right; and all are fever red on the thermometer of modern apocalypticism. Therefore, they constitute marching orders for the armies of righteousness. Let us trace this movement by way of our visual typology.

The ascent of the 1980s toward the kingdom (which God is bringing toward us on the destiny charts of the Right) begins in the same way as the pilgrims of the 1960s, with preachers and teachers. The counterpart of the activist clergy of that period is the contemporary electronic preacher. Apart from the obvious theological and political reversal, the big difference is the arming of this new corps of consciousness-raisers with the most sophisticated ideological weaponry. It has turned the technology of its apolitical predecessor from escapist to activist

purposes. Hence our first stick figure is portrayed on the living room screen.

The launching of the Moral Majority, Inc., in 1979, and thus the addition of an explicitly political instrument and purpose to the religious and moral urgings of Falwell's "Old Time Gospel Hour," is symbolic of a general swing by the Religious Right from exhortation to political action. Election year politics in 1980, the campaign to get out the vote among clergy and congregations by the Religious Right, and the activities of the Religious Roundtable and Christian Voice converged with this tendency. Unlike parallel movements in the 1960s, electoral politics preceded legislative action because the earlier movement was able to appeal to an existing charter (for example, the 1954 Supreme Court school desegregation ruling) for its visions, whereas the Religious Right first had to create the political documents to which adherence could be sought. Hence the strong pressure to elect "Christian politicians" who will implement the views of the moral majority.

With the changing of the political climate in 1980, and in particular the election to national office of prominent figures sympathetic with many of the goals of the Religious Right, it was not long before the predictable legislative stage was entered. The introduction of new laws—a comprehensive family bill, increased military spending, anti-abortion legislation—and resistance to changes removing laws which were seen as expressing the values of an earlier era (for example, the Equal Rights Amendment), along with a more general introduction of government policy reflecting the Religious Right's attitudes to work, welfare, environment, and international relations, embodied the intensification of this step.

Of course, no simple visual scheme can catch all the nuances here, and more aggressive political action has been dispersed throughout these first three steps. But logical and chronological development is visible in social change. We see such an evolution in the next predominant flurry of activity among the Religious Right: the onset of a public protest paralleling the advancing stage in the civil rights, poverty, and peace movements of the 1960s. Rallies, picketing, demonstrations, and boycotts have been organized, focusing on one or more issues important to the Religious Right and the New Right. A massive "Love America rally" in Washington was an early manifestation. A toughening of public posture comes with street demonstrations against a local bill for homosexual rights, picketing at a theatre showing an objectionable film, symbolic burning of books disapproved for reading in the public library, proposed economic boycott of products advertised on morally suspect television programs.[7]

We saw earlier that frustration of political purposes leads to the escalation of the methods of change agents. Will there be a movement beyond the legal methods used to date? Jerry Falwell has said publicly that he would endorse civil disobedience if women were drafted into the army.[8] Given the change in his views toward Martin Luther King's methods, it is possible that acts of nonviolence and civil disobedience will be entertained by the Religious Right, a violation of civil law under the claims of a higher moral law.

What about a thrust beyond violent protest against property and persons, random or instrumental? Scattered acts of property destruction have been carried out by militant anti-abortionists against abortion clinics. The paramilitary preparedness and paranoia of groups on the "hard" Radical Right are well known. However, there is no evidence of any movement in this direction among the Religious Right as we have defined it. The attraction of the leadership of the Religious Right to Martin Luther King's history and method of social change would argue for the unlikelihood of any call on their part to the course of violence. And the marginal ethos and often erratic life-style of yesterday's revolutionaries contrast sharply with the establishment status and values of most of the Religious Right. On the other hand, the latter are not ideological pacifists as was King. A situation perceived to be comparable to the tyranny of George III and the East India Tea Company would provoke a reaction in kind. We leave our visual aid with question marks indicating an unknown future.

To summarize, this is how the totality of struggles in the last decades from the darkness of the pit to light looks.

Furnished with some sense of the political, spiritual, and historical location of the Religious Right, we move now to the major questions of this study: What are its underlying theological premises? How are these to be assessed from the point of view of classical Christian faith?

CHAPTER 3

Sources and Norms
of Authority

Every theology is determined by the source or sources from
which it draws its ideas and the norm or norms which pass
final judgment on its view of reality. Debates within Christian
theology about the question of authority generally fix on three
claimants: the Scripture of the Old and New Testaments, the
teaching and thinking of the Christian community, and the experience and perceptions of human beings, moral, visceral, and
intellectual. Do all three enter into the formation of Christian
doctrine, or only one or two? If more than one, which source
takes precedence?[1]

In responding to these questions for the Religious Right,
we discover that answers must be sought at two levels: the
stated theological position of the Religious Right and an unstated view that covertly shapes its moral and political judgments. "By their fruits you shall know them." In this first doctrinal
inquiry we observe a tendency manifest throughout its teaching, the presence of both *explicit* and *implicit* theological
positions.

The explicit concept of authority in the Religious Right is
the Reformation principle *sola Scriptura*, Scripture alone. The
uniqueness of scriptural authority is interpreted in its most
radical form as "biblical inerrancy": the plenary verbal inspiration of the autographs and their protection from error in origin
and in transmission. This notion of authority means that in
matters of faith, morality, science, and history, Scripture (autho-

rized editions and translations) constitutes a single and trust-worthy source and norm for Christian doctrine.[2] The "plain meaning" which emerges from the pages of the Bible—its account of the beginning of the world and its vivid prophecies of the details of its ending, its complex chronologies and long genealogies, its conceptions of the status and role of women, its unified morality and theology—addresses us with one authoritative voice. This is the formal warrant for the Religious Right's position on the creationist-evolutionist and feminist controversies and its end-of-the-world apocalypticism.

We may visualize this theory of authority by means of the following chart:

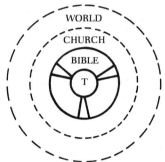

CHART 1

Truth (T) is found by rejecting the authority of church and world. Ecclesial tradition and human experience are untrustworthy by virtue of their sinful taint. So authority is the Bible, as signified by the solid lines of the inner circle, in its totality and perspicuity. Read at any point, the Bible gives the word of God on every subject.

We observed earlier that the Religious Right reserves its sharpest attacks for "secular humanism."[3] When it appears under Christian auspices ("liberal churches" or "liberation theology"), the authority structure of secular humanism may be visualized as in chart 2.

Another view of authority becomes visible when we look at the *implicit* doctrinal assumptions that pervade the thought of the Religious Right. Since we are speaking here of a source of authority which is not explicit, we identify it for the present

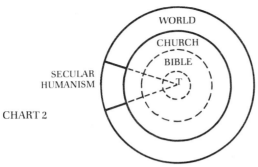

CHART 2

as an hypothesis to be tested as we work through the theological positions in subsequent chapters.

This second view is characterized by a functional *perspective* drawn from human experience, routed through one segment of church life and tradition, and making selective use of Scripture to validate its secular *source* and sectarian *resource*. To put it another way, strong evidence can be discerned of the controlling influence of secular premises, with ecclesiastical legitimations, in the theology and practice of the Religious Right. Ironically, a Religious Right which portrays its foes as under the domination of secular humanism is subject to the same charge. The difference is merely the segment of human experience—the cultural assumptions and political loyalties—which does the shaping. Furthermore, the religious passions of the right wing bear the mark of a wider human experience, a perennial perception of radical dualism which has found historical expression in such religions as Zoroastrianism and Manicheism. We shall trace the impact of these worldly factors in the doctrines of creation, fall, covenant, Christ, church, salvation, and consummation, and in the conception of God. A portrayal of this view of authority looks like this:

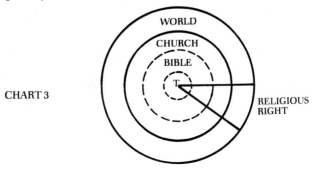

CHART 3

The continuing line of the world of human experience defines the source for the perspective arising on its right. A segment of the church—the radical Reformation and Christian dualism past and present—provides the resource refinements. Together these make their way through correlative sections of Scripture to establish the assertions of Truth.

The understanding of authority on the basis of which we shall analyze and assess the Religious Right in this book is that of classical Christianity. Seeking to honor each element for the role it has played in historic faith, it is thus "catholic" in its scope and "protestant" in its standard. The Scriptures constitute the source, the church the resource, and the world the setting for theological assertions. As the Bible is the Word of God addressed to us for the response of faith, its norm is Jesus Christ and the gospel. Behind this conception of authority lies an understanding of revelation as the Holy Spirit's disclosure of ultimate truth through God's acts centering on the incarnation and atonement, as discerned by the inspired prophetic and apostolic testimony of Scripture. But the work of the Spirit ranges throughout the world and the church, however challenged, distorted, and limited by sin and human finitude. These two orbits thus have their delimited role as resource and setting for the biblical and christological source and norm.

This alternative structure of authority can be portrayed in this manner:

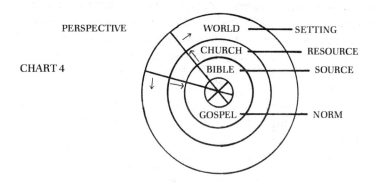

PERSPECTIVE   WORLD ——— SETTING

CHURCH ——— RESOURCE

CHART 4   BIBLE ——— SOURCE

GOSPEL ——— NORM

Beginning in the issues and idiom of a given time and place in human experience, this perspective acknowledges the need to listen for the work of the Spirit in the best of human experience in every historical context and recognizes that theology is influenced by the location and language of its period. But it passes these worldly dynamics through the critical test ring of the wisdom of the Christian community, its ancient teaching and contemporary perceptions. Finally it scrutinizes these claims by the test of the scriptural source and christological norms as represented by the Christ symbol and the solid inner line of the gospel story.

The dynamism pervading this process, however, is not adequately conveyed if we look only at the movement from the outer rings toward the center, for the affirmations of truth found in the Scripture also make their way out from the center to the periphery, seeking clarification in the church and translations in human experience. These in turn are to be defined and tested by the movement to the core. All the lines in this visualization are solid, indicating openness to the total biblical witness, the catholicity of church tradition, and the fulness of human experience. The arrows in the outer ring signify recurrent shifts of angle of vision from one historical situation to the next, always requiring fresh translations yet always accountable to the biblical and christological source and norms.

We believe this is how Christian doctrine has classically been developed and set forth, both in the past and in ecumenical faith in our own time. To give only one example, the borrowing of the Logos and homoousios concepts from the philosophical world contemporary with early Christianity and the passage of these through the refining fires of church thought and biblical redefinition provided a way of expressing the person of Christ in the great tradition.

The key question is always how the world's agenda and ideas comport or conflict with the biblical source and christological norm. At each point in our assessment of the Religious Right, we shall be seeking to answer that question.

CHAPTER 4

Creation

A highly charged item on the political agenda of the Religious Right whose theological relevance is obvious is "creationism."[1] In much of this first chapter of the Christian story, therefore, explicit rather than implicit doctrinal themes will be in the fore.

Briefly described, the doctrine of creation defended by the Religious Right is faithfulness to the Genesis accounts of cosmic beginnings. The first chapters of the Bible are seen as posing a direct challenge to "evolutionism," a theory of the inception of the universe which, the Religious Right asserts, eliminates God, bases its notion of the origin of species on false inferences from fossil data and other presumed geological evidence, and denies the unique status of humankind as made in the image of God. The creationist declares that the universe was made by God in the manner described in Genesis 1 and 2.

Less rigid interpreters among the Religious Right may consider the "days" of Genesis 1 as vast periods of time separating the stages of creation[2] ("a thousand years is as a day in the sight of the Lord"), while others, uncomfortable with such a metaphorical reading seek to make the case for a much shorter world history in conformity with biblical genealogies and chronologies. In either case, no development from one stage to the next is allowed, and such an idea is rejected with special vehemence with respect to the appearance of the human race. Each feature of creation came to be by divine fiat. At the crest of creation a literal Adam and Eve stepped forth in a locatable garden with its numinous tree and talking snake. Creationism supplies, in effect, a calendar, a map, and a cast of characters to understand the details of the world's beginning. In addition to the whys and wherefores, it requires information on the whos, hows, whens, and wheres. We shall observe a similar penchant for detail in the Religious Right's coverage of the world's end.

Creationism is taught in the science curriculums of the Christian academies supported by the Religious Right. Strong efforts are now being undertaken to insert a creationist view of the world's origins into public schools as well. Campaigns have been mounted to alter textbook and classroom presentations so as to identify evolution as theory rather than verified fact and to provide a second interpretation of origins in harmony with the creationist reading of Scripture.[3]

A view about human nature and its relationship to nature arises from this explicit teaching of the Religious Right. Let us look first at its anthropology, its doctrine of human nature.

In the Genesis account the Religious Right perceives the pre-eminence of Adam over against the other aspects of creation. Human beings are given dominion over nature. Trees are for lumber, minerals for energy, wildlife for human needs and uses. Moreover, the derivation of Eve from Adam's rib (Gen. 2:21—24) implies the subservience of women to men. Inferences drawn from other biblical texts are combined with this passage to establish the role of woman as that of helpmate to man, the bearer of children and the maker of the home. Femininity, maternity, and domesticity constitute the appropriate life-style of women. Feminism, the struggle for equal rights, and the movement of women into the work world are considered direct attacks on the divinely established position of the female sex in the order of creation.

The Religious Right holds explicitly that humanity is made in the image of God (Gen. 1:27). In large part its controversy with evolutionism grows out of this belief in the singular claim and capacity of human beings, a claim and capacity that it is convinced is destroyed by the evolutionist's emphasis on the continuities between animal and human life. The image of God refers to the special relation God has with the creature with the human face and the uniquely human spiritual capacities—freedom, choice, reason, and will.

The Religious Right's strong commitment to the doctrine of creation in the image of God is expressed not only in the debate with evolutionists, but also in moral and religious judgments and religious practices. Its stress on the moral life, on loyalty to the ten commandments, and on obedience to divine and human law all presuppose that humanity has the capacity to be obedient and keep the law, since all people are made in God's image. The other side of this emphasis is seen in the condemnation the Religious Right calls down on those who do not choose the good. There are stern judgments for those whose economic condition is seen as a failure of the moral will—the chronically unemployed are readily described as lazy, and many if not most welfare recipients are categorized as "chiselers." Similarly, criminals are not to be excused by social conditions and should be seen instead as responsible objects of retributive justice.

The same intense focus on the exercise of the God-given gift of free choice is reflected in the revivalist traditions of the Religious Right. One comes to faith by a once-and-for-all-time decision, and out of this moment of regeneration comes the continuing challenge to the disciplines of the moral and spiritual life, requiring great exertions of the will. The theology of the Religious Right, like that of orthodox Protestantism, understands both the justification of the sinner and the sanctification of the believer as a gift of grace through and through. But the practice of the Religious Right underscores the urgencies of choice, an anomaly which characterizes revivalist forms of Christianity and has historically come to expression in the Arminian-Calvinist disagreement. Our point here is simply that the altar calls of the camp meeting and stadium revival fit in with the Religious Right's emphasis on the proper use of the freedom given to all in creation.

Again, following orthodox theology, the Religious Right holds that human beings, though singularly made in the image of God, share the status of creaturehood with the rest of creation. Creatureliness means derivation from deity and implies physi-

cality. "The Lord God formed man of dust from the ground
. . ." (Gen. 2:7a). As such, the spirit is intimately associated with
the body: "The Lord God breathed into his nostrils the breath
of life; and man became a living being" (Gen. 2:7b). Here and in
related texts (such as Gen. 2:23 – 24) are warrants for the long-
standing Christian belief in the goodness of creation and the
inherent dignity of the body. Thus the unity of body and soul
and physical dignity are entailed in these Genesis texts so important to the creationist. In the section following we shall
assess how this formal adherence to traditional Christian
teaching matches the Religious Right's working assumptions
about freedom of the will and the status of the body.

ASSESSMENT

Yes. The Religious Right is loyal to the Christian tradition in its
view that the world, life, and human life are brought to be by
Another. "Secular humanist" notions about cosmic and human
origins that are introduced either overtly or covertly into evolutionary hypotheses are clearly contrary to the classical Christian doctrine of creation. Notions of origin that speak of chance,
accident, or spontaneous generation, are competing philosophical perspectives on creation to be opposed as firmly as
early Christian theology rejected fate and fortune as explanations of the world's origin and development. Scientific accounts
ought to make clear the crucial distinction between their data
and interpretations on the one hand and the philosophical and
theological frameworks into which those data and interpretations can be placed on the other.

In its creationist argument the Religious Right makes another valid point (which does not bear directly on our present
concern)—the difference between scientifically verifiable evidence and theories projected from that data base which seek
to lend coherence to the evidence. "Evolution" is such a theory,
formulated to make sense of the data. The great majority of
those who work most closely with the evidence find arguments
for the theory of evolution persuasive, and alternative interpretations have yet to gain any credibility in the scientific com-

munity. However, the status of evolution as a theory cannot be denied.

On the explicit doctrine of human nature, the Religious Right is faithful to the Christian teaching regarding both the creatureliness of human beings and the divine image in them. The assertion that Adam—humankind—is unique within creation is an indisputable article of faith. In the image of God human beings are conferred with a special dignity and provided with the capacity to respond to its attendant call.

No. If we employ the concept of biblical authority set forth on page 36 to interpret the Christian view of creation, we uncover a fundamental confusion in the Religious Right's teaching. Classical Christianity, by what it has *not* said, as well as by what it has said, lifts up certain teachings as integral to the narrative of faith. The creation of the world by God is propelled to the foreground of the doctrine of creation ("I believe in God the Father Almighty, Maker of heaven and earth . . ."; "We believe in one God the Father Almighty, Maker of heaven and earth, and of all things visible and invisible . . ."),[4] as is the implication that the created order is good. The Christian position, in controversies with early Gnostics, neo-Platonists, and Manicheans, and their counterparts today, denies that the world is either inferior or illusory because it came to be from God's own creative act. On the other hand, it is not to be elevated to the status of deity, as is done by those who divinize or romanticize the created order. The doctrine of creation holds that the material and temporal world is good but not God, to be honored but not to be worshiped. The affirmation of divine creation denies the notions of self-generation, accidental origin, and creation by demonic forces or subsidiary deities. It sets the world in the context of a great purpose and plan, life together with God, the community of creation with Creator.

These themes concerning the purpose and goal of creation recur throughout the catechesis, worship, mission, and apologetics of the Christian tradition. They represent a christological and evangelical sifting of the Genesis accounts of creation, the Word amidst the words, the gospel for which the book of good news is written. The general affirmations become particular in the Christian understanding of nature and human nature. With respect to nature the good creation is affirmed, enjoyed, tended, and investigated in sacramental and covenantal ways that run counter to the negativity expressed in other religious traditions. And human life is prized as the apple of God's eye by virtue of its creation in the divine image.

This first chapter of the Christian narrative is told in the Scriptures with the materials at hand to the early storytellers. As such it includes the beliefs about the how, the when, the where, and the who of the cosmos which people of that time and place held. That is perfectly fitting for the God of this story, who works in and with the time and matter of the good earth to reveal divine truth through the vehicles of finitude rather than ignoring, denying, or working around them.

But the gift of the divine truth cannot be confused with its earthly wrappings. Passing notions of how, where, when, and who are not to be mistaken for the abiding declarations of why and wherefore. Such a confusion results when an "ism"—creationism—is substituted for the classical Christian doctrine of creation, when an early theory of how the world came to be, as transient as the flat-earth and three-story-universe hypotheses also found in Scripture, is taken as gospel teaching. To make this move is to fuse a secular cosmology, born of and appropriate to a particular time and place, with fundamental affirmations of the Christian faith. Not only does this muddle the church's theology, but it also weakens its preaching, teaching, evangelism, and apologetics. Those tasks require us to take as seriously in our own time what the authors of Scripture did in theirs: the need to put the gospel in the language and thought forms of our own day. While the inordinate claims of evolutionary theory deserve a rebuke, the proper task of Christian proclamation is creatively to relate the best scientific thought of its own day to the ancient themes of Christian doctrine.

While bearing more on Christian ethics than systematic theology, a comment is in order here on the effort of the Religious Right to add creationist theory to public school textbooks. It is appropriate to protest the covert insertion of secularist theories of the world's origin into evolutionary accounts in the teaching of science. But two wrongs do not make a right. Public school teachers have no business expounding theology. The separation doctrine must be taken seriously. For the public school system even to state what theological views on this subject are available is itself to take a theological position and therefore inappropriate for text or teaching. (The followers of the Catholic palaeontologist Pierre Teilhard de Chardin, for example, would clearly reject the simple alternatives of creationism versus evolutionism, as would many other points of view.)

We move now from the issues surrounding the interpretation of the biblical accounts of creation to specific doctrinal questions about nature and human nature. Here we confront both explicit teaching by the Religious Right and implicit assumptions behind its moral and political judgments and religious practices. In spite of its loudly proclaimed defense of the Genesis account of creation, the Religious Right deviates sharply from these in its environmental politics. Classical Christianity has developed a doctrine of the dignity of material things and their beneficent interrelationships in opposition to dualistic world views which either disdain subhuman creation or pit human nature against nature. How is this teaching from Scripture and tradition treated in the legislation and government and corporate policies recommended by the supporters of the Religious Right? The programs of U.S. Interior Secretary James Watt, a representative of the Religious Right with power in government, demonstrate a functional theology which differs from the professed Christian orthodoxy. In the use of government lands for the pursuit of private profit, in the treatment of animal life, in proposed limitations on setting aside land for the preservation and enjoyment of the environment, and in public statements about the transiency of material phenomena, another point of view is being set forth.[5] The doctrine implied by such policies bears little resemblance to the stewardship of natural resources, the tending of animal life, the nurture of mutually supported relationships between nature and human nature, in short to the ecological ethic that rises out of the Christian doctrine of creation.

To be sure, part of the Christian ecological ethic has to do with the rights of humanity in creation and the invitation to use natural resources for human welfare. But the cultivation of the fruits of creation is a far cry from their exploitation. Making nature subservient to the purposes of economic profit violates not only the inherent dignity of nature, but in the long run destroys human welfare also.[6] In both theory and practice we find here a dualism in the line of Gnostic and Manichean thought. Classical Christianity set itself against these world views in the early centuries. The struggle continues. Human nature and nature are partners in creation, not competitors, both sharing in the goodness of God's original intention and in the glorified life together of God's final purpose, the kingdom of God set in the environment of a new heaven and a new earth.

The second-class status of nature is also revealed in the Religious Right's consistent association of sin with the "lusts of the flesh." Time and again the body is cast in the role of the enemy. This expression of dualism is more appropriately dealt with under the rubric of the fall, but we allude to it here as pinpointing nature as the prime subject of fallibility.

The crown of nature is human nature. And its most precious jewel is "man." That is, humanity in its highest expression, if we judge according to how the doctrine of the Religious Right functions in the political, social, and moral realms, is *masculine* humanity. "Equal rights" are inappropriate for the other half of the human race, as the campaign against the Equal Rights Amendment attests. The woman must be subservient to the man in the home, in the affairs of the world, and in the church. Thus the image of God, operationally, as the warrant for dignity and as embodied in the function of rationality, comes to highest expression in the male of the human species, in contrast to the inferior functions of body and emotion in the female.

This implicit and explicit teaching of the Religious Right is contrary to the theology of Genesis 1: "God created man in his own image; male and female created he them. And God blessed them ..." (Gen. 1:27, 28a). It also disputes the doctrine of equality in sexual creation as set forth in Paul's christological norm: "There is neither Jew nor Greek, there is neither slave nor free, there is neither male nor female; for you are all one in Christ Jesus" (Gal. 3:28).[7] The specific application of the hierarchical view to the status of women in the church, especially the ordination of women, has now been vigorously challenged by biblical scholarship, including evangelical scholarship.[8] Here again we observe that a doctrinal position drawn from cultural opinions and colored by the dualistic assumptions of other religions exercises a controlling influence in the outlook of the Religious Right.

The stress on freedom in the anthropology of the Religious Right bears close inspection. As mentioned earlier, the classical understanding interrelates the image of God and the creaturely condition of human beings. Physical and spiritual dimensions live in dynamic unity. The location of the spirit in this matrix of space and time means that the realities of this world make their impact felt on the spiritual life. But does the Religious Right's functional doctrine of human nature recognize and acknowledge this home of the spirit in the body and the body's environment of collective forces and institutions? In the way it distributes both moral expectations and moral censure, the Religious Right addresses the self as if it were a pure spirit with no supportive or inhibiting physical connectedness. There is no recognition that the privileges of the healthy and the rich grant them a freedom not enjoyed by the poor, whose ability to choose is constricted by the social and economic factors which affect their finitude. Here is a profound and critical failure to see that humans live at the "juncture of nature and spirit" and not in the realm of pure spirit.[9]

Because freedom is related to a finitude which either capacitates or incapacitates, biblical judgments are harsher on the rich:[10] "To whom much is given, of him will much be required" (Luke 12:49). Turning this principle on its head, the Religious Right frequently excoriates the poor for not pulling themselves up by their own celestial bootstraps and wants to deny them the economic supports which would fortify them for their proper moral reach. But rich or poor, human beings are not the disembodied spirits of a dualistic religion but creatures who dwell at the intersection of the traffic of finitude and infinity.[11]

CHAPTER 5

Fall

The second chapter of the Christian story tells about the fist shaken in the face of the Creator God. Invited at creation into responsive relationship with its Maker, the world chooses instead to go its own way. It turns from God, stumbles and falls. Now the whole of creation is distanced from its source, fractured in its life, in bondage to its own willfulness.

This fundamental Christian teaching about the rebellion of the human race and the destruction it brings on itself is preached and believed by the Religious Right. The reality of human sin is brought home forcefully to the believer in the evangelical experience of repentance and conversion. The literal accounts of humankind's first fall, when the serpent successfully beguiled Adam and Eve in the Garden of Eden, vividly portray the universal estrangement from God. The righteous God who provided this period of probation for our primal parents holds us accountable for this rebellion. In most interpretations of original sin in the Religious Right, the poisons of their disobedience in Genesis 3 are passed down the line through procreation to all humanity. We all stand accused by a just God, deserving of a punishment that fits the crime, the eternal fires of hell. This is the teaching of the Religious Right on the fall, its explicit doctrine of sin.

Another perspective on the human condition arises from the political positions and programs of the Religious Right, and is related to its form of piety. This second, covert view is less suspicious of universal human nature and positively sanguine about the possibilities of one segment of it.

Representative of this second view is the philosophy and activity of Moral Majority, Inc., whose very name suggests a fundamental division between human beings based on the idea that some practice the law of righteousness and are therefore "moral," while others violate that law and are therefore immoral.[1] To all intents and purposes the doctrine of universal sin is abandoned. The dividing line which the Religious Right draws in its explicit theology between all sinners in their fallen state and God the righteous judge is moved: it becomes the line between the morally upright and the immorally fallen. The human problem is no longer the controversy God has with the rebellious race as a whole, but the controversy the moral majority has with the immoral minority.

A significant clue to this other doctrine of the fall is the political approach of the Religious Right. High on its agenda is the election and support of "Christian politicians" or righteous public officials. In effect these people are seen as exempt from the taint of sin and therefore trustworthy rulers. Conjoined to this is the search for the "mighty man" in politics, business, and religion, into whose hands we can place decisions. The acquisition of profit and the administration of wealth by the righteous industrialist are to be encouraged. Confidence is placed in those who wield power (so long as they are of the moral majority), whether this be trust in the male hierarchy of the family or pastoral hegemony in a local congregation. These chosen ones do not share in the corruptibility to which human nature in general is subject.[2]

The same abyss separating the righteous and the unrighteousness within the nation is seen also between the nation and the nations. Just as sin clings to some of the citizenry and virtue to others, so evil comes to focus in the unrighteous nation and good in the righteous one. The Soviet Union and the United States are, of course, the manifestations of this dualism.

This division between the moral and the immoral is not, for Moral Majority, Inc. (although it is for other segments of the Religious Right), the same as the line between the true and false religious believer. The "reverse ecumenism" to which we referred earlier is at work in the doctrine of the fall, for the righteous may include Mormons, Jews, Roman Catholics, and other people of good will who do not subscribe to the tenets of Protestant fundamentalism or share the born-again experience of the Religious Right. What is influential in the stark division between moral and immoral, nevertheless, is the background of the born-again experience, which draws a sharp distinction between "we" and "they." The agony and ecstasy of the conversion experience lead some to conclude that they are now free from sin, having a righteousness *totally imparted* as well as *totally imputed,* in contrast to those who are not twice-born and are thus without the pale.

ASSESSMENT

Yes. Adherence to the second chapter of the Christian story in its overt teaching is a mark of faithfulness in the theology of the Religious Right. The biblical narrative asserts this world's rejection of its Maker's invitation. The fall is *the* problematic in the Christian narrative, a radical reversal of the divine purposes. This deep-seated state of rebellion is expressed in the universal tendency to seek first the interest of the self rather than the kingdom of God, in the alienation within creation and between creation and the Creator. The personal knowledge of this enmity that comes in the experience of repentance and conversion is a grace given to those of evangelical piety, which makes abstract theological talk about our universal state of bondage to sin existential.

No. Where we might be led to expect the greatest contribution of the Religious Right because of its realism about human nature we find the greatest disappointment. In place of a resolute application of this Christian teaching to political issues, another view of human nature intrudes. This second perspective eliminates sobriety about the universal state of sin in favor of a naïveté about the human condition. Because of the apocalyptic framework of the theology of the Religious Right, this naïveté goes beyond that of secular humanism, with which it shares this illusion. The Religious Right elevates the distinction between an untainted "we" and a tainted "they" to Armageddon-like proportions. Its functional doctrine of the fall departs from the Christian story and takes up a tale in line with the dualistic religious traditions of Zoroastrianism and Manicheism.

Let us look first at the alteration of the formal doctrine of the fall. In orthodox thought no exceptions are made to the universal taint. The state of sin and its expression in the willfulness of the human spirit persist to the end, no matter how much their consequences may be altered before God by the grace of justification or modified in the believer's life by the grace of sanctification. In fact biblical realism about sin is particularly sensitive to the dangers of claiming too much for the achievements of virtue and piety. Hence the judgment rendered on the self-righteous who proclaim, "God, I thank thee I am not like other men" (Luke 18:11). Before God "all our righteous deeds are like a polluted garment" (Isa. 64:6). In the Christian narrative the fundamental rift is not between the presumed righteous and the unrighteous but between the holy God and the rebellious world. Whatever righteousness does exist is imputed by God's gracious declaration of pardon, not achieved by moral virtuosity. Later we shall explore the implications of this for the Religious Right's doctrine of salvation.

The outworking of this utter honesty about human nature is a wariness within Scripture and the Christian tradition about the accumulation of power, whether it be the moral and spiritual power which tempted the Pharisee, the economic power of the rich, the intellectual power of the wise, or the political power of the ruler. Because of the temptations of ascending power planted by the universal self-regarding inclinations, "power tends to corrupt and absolute power corrupts absolutely," as Lord Acton said. The Religious Right's confidence in the "mighty man" goes absolutely contrary to this basic insight into the corruptibility of power. The presumed exemption from the baleful effects of the will to power on the part of the mighty moral politician, the mighty moral industrialist, the mighty moral minister, and the mighty moral nation is a dangerous political and social illusion. The evangelist Luke records the song of Jesus' mother, who expresses the pervasive biblical theme that the Lord "has put down the mighty from their thrones, and exalted those of low degree" (1:52).

The translation of the biblical wisdom about human nature into political strategies entails the restraint not the release of the powerful. Historically this was one of the salutary influences of biblical faith on America's charters. The separation of powers into legislative, executive, and judicial presupposes the corruptibility of power as the nation's founders experienced it in political and religious forms. The pyramiding of authority in an established religion, hierarchally organized, and the concentration of power in political office would not be repeated on this side of the Atlantic. The separation of church and state and the balance of the three branches within the state represent the political realism that grows out of a grasp of the frailties of human nature.[3]

In the American experience, caution about the concentration of power includes checks and balances. Standing in the classical tradition which views the authority of the state as a means of setting bounds to the harm sinful humanity can do, American government includes not only the civil function of law and order but the restraint of the imperial drives of economic power. And it has sought through means of responsible government not only to bring "the mighty from their thrones" but also to exalt "those of low degree."

The irony we meet in the Religious Right is its opposition—in theology and policy—to these fundamental Christian themes and their outworking in the American experience. Here is a contradiction of the very religious and political values to which such vociferous allegiance is given. Power is self-consciously pyramided, trust is placed in those whose moral credentials are seen as implying a right to use it. Thus the dangers of concentrated power are lost upon the Religious Right. This is so with one exception: government as such is regularly suspect. Those who govern least are thought to govern best. But this exception only underscores the irony, for the protest is directed against government at precisely those points where it has sought to do justice to biblical realism about the corruptibility of the strong and to the Magnificat's espousal of the cause of the weak. The Religious Right wants to remove restraints from the powerful, confident that their native goodness will not be a threat to the weak, and supports from the weak, on the grounds of the notion of human freedom we examined in the last chapter.

Thus the Christian doctrines of creation and fall are both rendered inoperative in the moral and political policies of the Religious Right. In their place is put a concept of the perfectibility of human nature which is in direct continuity with the Enlightenment view that produced contemporary "secular humanism." In the case of the Religious Right, the enlightenment of human beings is located in the religious experience of conversion rather than the secular experience of education, but the optimistic expectations about one sector of the human race are the same—as is the departure from the Christian tradition.

As we said, this "humanistic" view of moral perfectibility is expressed in dramatic terms within the context of the piety of the Religious Right. Fervor escalates the rhetoric, and the expectation of the imminent end of the world places the cast of characters in this moral drama on the stage of cosmic history. The armies of righteousness and unrighteousness are arrayed against each other, ready for the final conflict. The world in which we live, as embodied in the current political strife, is a place of apocalyptic struggle. This is a cosmic contest, God being on one side and Satan on the other. Later we shall see how this conception affects other doctrines, especially eschatology; here we note its implication for the doctrine of the fall.

To interpret contemporary political and moral engagement as a battle between light and darkness is a concept of human nature and history as old as Zoroastrianism.[4] This teaching of Zarathustra developed into a religion which at one time covered a large section of the Near East, and its influence was felt in Judaism as it came in contact with Persian culture after the Exile. Dualism appeared in another form in the third century after Christ as Manicheism, which made significant inroads into Christianity. For eight years early in his life Augustine was an adherent of this doctrine, and a case can be made that the spirit and some forms of Manicheism persisted within Christianity throughout the Middle Ages.[5]

The teaching and practice of the Religious Right show overwhelming evidence of the continuation of this other religious tradition. A provisional dualism and drama are as much part of Christian faith as they are of Zoroastrianism and Manicheism. But in Christianity the battle is waged between a holy God and the whole creation captive to the powers of sin, evil, and death. The line is not drawn between two armies within the world, with the clear insignias of moral good and moral evil, but between the great grey army of the world and its solitary Opponent. Indeed, within the world there is a community which represents the one who contests the power of darkness, which is called out to hear the word and see the light, to turn toward it and to walk in it. But even this Dawn People cast their shadows in the world. Sin persists in the lives of the elect whose very profession of faith is signaled by a confession of sin, of membership in the immoral majority. They know that "none is righteous, no, not one" (Rom. 3:10). And the vulnerability of the "righteous" to the worst sin of all, spiritual pride, makes any conception of a dualism between the righteous and the unrighteousness impossible.

We shall examine other distinctions between Christian faith and the Zoroastrian mentality in connection with subsequent doctrines: the providence that is free to use the unrighteous as an instrument of the divine purpose, thus qualifying the dualism of righteous and unrighteous; the defeat of the power of evil in the royal work of Christ, which mitigates the dualist's anxieties about the powers of Satan; the classic Christian view of the end of all things, as distinguished from the technicolor scenarios of the Religious Right. But one other motif, a soteriological one, deserves mention here. The sharp distinction associated with some interpretations of the conversion experience may contribute to an uncritical dualism. The trauma of the new birth is sometimes mistaken for the adulthood of faith. The "delivery experience" becomes so absorbing that the need for growth is lost from view. Soteriology is confused with eschatology: what is only a beginning is mistaken for arrival at the end point; justification and a struggling sanctification is mistaken for glorification. Thus the "already/not-yet" paradox of Christian faith, the element of having while not yet having, is obscured from view by a too-easy assurance of special moral and spiritual status. This fuels the fires of the dualistic imagination, making for a moralistic self-congratulation and a simplistic division between the forces of light and darkness.

The teaching about the transmission of human sin through procreation and the political preoccupation with sins related to sexuality evidence a conception of the fall closer to the Manichean and Gnostic points of view than to the classical Christian doctrine of sin. The Christian tradition relates sin to the twin dimensions of human selfhood: the image of God and its spiritual capacity, and human creatureliness and its biological and physical reality—the sins of pride and concupiscence. However, the sin of pride is fundamental, the lust for godlike power chronicled in the Genesis story. The willingness of the Religious Right to trust the powerful undercuts sensitivity to the dangers of the arrogance of power. And the regular association of sin with sexuality, for all its appropriate concern about contemporary promiscuity, too easily overlooks the more serious roots of sin in the pretensions of the spirit. In so doing the Religious Right again sounds a note more in harmony with the ascetic and anti-physical spirituality of traditional dualism than with Christian belief.

PROVIDENCE

A narrative interpretation of Christian faith goes on at this point to introduce the doctrine of providence. After the fall a grace of preservation is at work in God's creation. This universal care will not allow the world to fall back into nonbeing. God's tender mercies are over all his works; human rebellion does not turn aside the divine determination.

Providence so understood at this point in the story (its meaning will be enriched by subsequent events) is the being and action of the God who sets boundaries to the destructive impulses and effects of the fall. This providential care chastens the wicked, supports the weak, and directs the lives and destinies of persons and nations toward the divine purposes. It is the general grace of God as it keeps life human, sustains the earth, and makes for wholeness in all of creation. Providence is as personal as the intimations of conscience and as corporate as the judgments of history and the laws of nature.

This right ordering of the world under providence involves what have been called "orders of preservation"—the state, human work, the family. Through them life is made livable: its essentials are supplied and the potential of existence is nourished. To the orders of general preservation are joined the insights of general revelation. Humanity is given enough light to see its way through the darkness of a fallen world. Sufficient reflection is preserved in the divine image in us, though shattered by the fall, to illumine the path. Our moral sensibilities, our religious intuitions, our intellectual gropings, however misdirected by original sin, are reliable enough to discern the direction we must go. For all that, the one with whom we have to do, and the true Way, are hidden from us by the consequences of our sin. Nevertheless, the testimony to providence in its general care of a fallen world is part and parcel of the Christian story.

Many of these themes are affirmed in the teaching of the Religious Right. God watches over the world, even in the very smallest of its details. The effects of sin are modified by the orders of preservation. One hears frequent references to Romans 13 as a biblical endorsement of the state, with the accent placed on its functions of promulgating law and maintaining order. Economic life is conceived to be under the direction of God. In fact, the Bible is seen as providing very specific guidance: "The free enterprise system is clearly outlined in the Book of Proverbs in the Bible. Jesus Christ made it clear that the work ethic was a part of His plan for man. Ownership of property is biblical. Ambitious and successful business management is clearly outlined as part of God's plan for His people."[6] And of course, the family has been a high priority on the agenda of the Religious Right from the outset.

The Religious Right grants the validity of general revelation in its support for moral and political coalitions with those who do not share their Christian orthodoxy. The approval of the ideals of America's founding fathers—though some of them were clearly deists rather than orthodox Christians—is another recognition of the significance of a divine grace that sheds light and life beyond the bounds of special Christian revelation.

A very strong commitment to the providential ordering of the affairs of nations is held by the Religious Right. Often quoted is the biblical proverb that "righteousness exalts a nation, but sin is a reproach to any people" (Prov. 14:34). God blesses those states that live by the light of the moral laws of general revelation and the orders of preservation, and rains down judgment on nations which violate these laws and orders. This firm belief in God's justice, the blessings and curses that follow obedience and disobedience, lies behind the political imperatives of the Religious Right. It also expresses itself in a theocratic impulse. The laws of righteousness executed by righteous rulers is the way to guarantee a righteous nation.[7]

Here too we find unstated as well as stated convictions about providence. Sometimes the two converge, with the explicit teaching giving further rationale for the implicit—sometimes they pull in different directions. Coherent with the Religious Right's explicit views on the economic order is an implicit conception of how providence works. The belief that restraints should be removed from the ambitious entrepreneur is joined to the confidence that this will work for the benefit of the whole society, including the weak and the poor. Providence is trusted to order the many quests for economic gain in such a way that all will prosper. An "Invisible Hand" (Adam Smith) will carry out this beneficent work.

Related to this (but comporting less clearly with the Religious Right's explicit teaching on the function of government as an order of preservation against sin) is criticism of government as such and a fear of its presence and influence. The "least is best" philosophy of government manifests itself in the campaigns of the Religious Right against the size of government and its various programs for the general welfare. While the general literature of the Religious Right does not go so far as the statement in the *Blue Book* of the John Birch Society that "the greatest enemy of man is, and always has been government,"[8] the general assault on the presence of government in the affairs of the nation often bears practical resemblance to this extreme.

ASSESSMENT

Yes. The belief in providence as divinely ordering the world in the face of human destructiveness is part of the Christian narrative. Again, a concern with the order of preservation and thanksgiving to God for these civilizing forms, and accountability to God for the right stewardship of them, constitute a strong plank in the program of the Religious Right. Righteousness *does* exalt a nation and unrighteousness *does* destroy it. The economic order is accountable to God. The family is a divinely instituted design, and the weakening of it through promiscuity and ideological attack are deplorable. These elementary norms, which make and keep life human, are accessible through general revelation. Persons and nations who turn away from this light will find themselves in the darkness. God metes out justice to those who rend the fabric that providence so carefully preserves.

The Religious Right has biblical warrants for its wariness about the pretensions of government. Revelation 13, with its vision of the beast, must be held in tension with Romans 13. When the state becomes demonic, it must be resisted, as the early Christians did when they refused obedience to Rome. God's good gifts to us, including the very orders of preservation, can be corrupted by sin.

No. Serious departures from the Christian story are to be found in some of the explicit and implicit teachings of the Religious Right on the doctrine of providential preservation. We shall return to this in Chapter 11, where we give fuller attention to the doctrine of God.

The rationale for government as it is seen in this chapter of the story is to restrain the imperial drives of human sin and assure the well-being of human life together in a fallen world.

Efforts to remove these restraints and to release the impulses of self-aggrandizement and ambitious profiteering controvert the very purposes of governance. This permissiveness unleashes a destructive will to power which is the epitome of human sin. The political order of preservation exists to protect human beings from this, not to license it. Those laws and policies in the American tradition which protect the weak from avarice, support the victims of its deleterious effects, and control the dominating tendencies of the strong are extensions of the biblical concept of governance. When the Religious Right attempts to eliminate such laws and reverse such policies, it does so out of a concept of the political order which is alien to the Christian tradition.

The shape of this alienation becomes clearer when a religious endorsement of a specific form of the economic order is added to the rejection of the biblical concept of the political order. While Scripture and Christian tradition regularly view the world of work as a divine mandate, they do not confuse this general mandate with a specific human theory of how that order is to be executed, be it capitalist or socialist. The doctrine of the sovereignty of God in itself prevents the Christian narrative from deifying any human construct. Under the rubric of the orders of preservation, the weight of classical Christian tradition is solidly against any simplistic identification of human economic theory with divine intentions. But if the Christian faith cannot be domesticated by any human economic fabrications, its christological and evangelical norms have clear economic implications. Christ began his ministry with the announcement of good news for the poor, preached neighbor love for the victim, excoriated the rich, and pointed to the kingdom of God in which justice would be done and peace made.[9] This vision cannot be easily made over into the image of a capitalist entrepreneur. The inclination of the Religious Right to do so is one more intrusion of the secular humanist view—in a right-wing political and economic form—into Christian theology.

The Religious Right's conception of providence evidences the replacement of Christian doctrine by notions imported from the secular arena. Its confidence that an invisible hand will oversee the release of the acquisitive instincts in society means that God will aid the mighty in their ascent to economic power. How does this view comport with the biblical declaration that God puts down the mighty from their thrones?

CHAPTER 6

Covenant

From the universal providence of God, which sustains and preserves all of creation from its self-destructive tendencies, we move to a particular channel in the history of divine action. In this stream of events God focuses on a special people to effect the eternal purpose. They are to be the agent of the world's liberation from the powers that hold it in thrall, the medium of its reconciliation. With Israel God has a covenant: God shall be their God and they shall be God's people. Delivered from bondage and brought to a land flowing with milk and honey, Israel is given not only a taste of God's Promised Land but also a vision of the *shalom* for which the world was made. The laws of that life together are set forth in the imperatives of the decalogue, in the wisdom of the sages, and in the hopes of the prophets. The covenant love which will not let this people go, even in the face of their rebellious response, finds the fulfilment of its promises in this people's chief prophet, priest, and king.

All these traditional themes are found in the teaching of the Religious Right. Israel and the Hebrew Scriptures play a prominent role in its faith. Signs of this loyalty to the Old Testament can be seen in the Religious Right's interpretation of the cosmological and theological assertions of the Genesis accounts of creation and fall. Equally important are the moral injunctions found in the Scriptures of the Hebrew people. The ten commandments and other Old Testament legal passages figure heavily in the Religious Right's views on capital punishment, abortion, sexuality, and family relationships. It cites Old

Testament judgments on righteous warfare, national responsibility to God, the discipline of children, the status and role of men and women, and the divine judgment on homosexuality in justifying its political programs. Considerable emphasis falls on those portions of the Old Testament which accent the divine holiness and human accountability to God's righteous wrath.[1]

The theory and practice of the Religious Right disclose another aspect of its view of God's covenant—Judaism today, particularly in the state of Israel. Since Israel has a special place in God's plan, the Religious Right is continually scrutinizing events in Jewish history. Thus the covenant with Israel continues in some sense, even though the church as the New Israel has replaced it in the economy of salvation.[2] The role Israel now plays, however, is as the subject and object of events that are preliminary to the last things: the conversion of some Jews, the return of this people of God to its homeland, its persecutions, the relation of the state of Israel to its foes are seen to be of special theological importance.[3] We shall return to this area in the discussion of eschatology in Chapter 10.

Another concept of covenant appears alongside that set forth in the Religious Right's understanding of the Jews. While not given overt theological explanation, it has covert theological weight. Precedents for this idea can be discovered in the Puritan tradition and in American civil religion: the notion that the United States of America has been chosen by God to play a unique role in the divine plan and is thus called to obey this covenant expectation.[4] At its inception America was given a vision of the true ideals of nationhood, especially that of freedom. Throughout its history it has had the special guidance of God. Today "the greatest nation in the world" is called to defend freedom against Communist encroachment. Its covenant status makes loyalty to America of a piece with loyalty to God. The convergence of these loyalties is to be recognized in ritual acts such as prayer in the public schools, national days of fasting and prayer, support for American military might, and the rooting out of secular humanism and the decadence it causes in the internal life of the nation.[5]

ASSESSMENT

Yes. The Hebrew Bible constitutes two-thirds of Christian Scripture. Classical Christian faith has regularly had to struggle against the temptation to follow the Marcionite reduction and scissor the Old Testament out of the Christian Bible and theology. The Religious Right is determined to honor the place of the Old Testament and the role of the people of Israel. From the covenantal stream that runs from Abraham through Moses to Jesus, Israel is God's elect in both promise and fulfilment. The law and the prophets do express the vision of *shalom* given to the elect. The moral rigor of the Old Testament has a place in Christian ethics. The love of God to which Christians point is a *holy* love which holds us responsible for violating it.

On both ethical and theological grounds the Religious Right's concern for the destiny of Jews today is commendable. The Religious Right is a potential ally to the Jewish people and the general community of conscience in the struggle against a re-emerging anti-Semitism. Its support is of special value because it is from the extreme right that this virulent prejudice has often come in the past. Indeed some who strongly agree on many other matters with the Religious Right feel particularly betrayed by the latter's friendly relations with Jews and with the state of Israel.[6]

The Religious Right's practical and political interest in the destiny of the Jews is another theological strength. This preoccupation gives Israel a continuing role in God's plan for which there is no equivalent in traditional displacement theories. As a matter of fact, the formal fundamentalist theology of the Religious Right espouses substitution of the old Israel by the church, in effect disenfranchising Jews from their divine election, but its apocalyptic political tendencies restore them to a significant place in the Christian drama. Paul's refusal to disqualify Israel from its special role, evident from his struggling in Romans 9 – 11, receives some acknowledgment from the Religious Right, though within the framework of a detailed eschatology.

The United States is a nation under God. Its charters and

traditions recognize this. Christians who understand the state as an order of preservation will view their country as under the divine purview and accountable to the divine imperatives. Its relationship is thereby covenantal, enjoying the promises of God's providential care and its corresponding duties.

No. Scripture is the word of God as it bears witness to Jesus Christ and the gospel. These christological and evangelical norms—the story and its central character—apply throughout the Bible. The writers of the New Testament cited and interpreted texts from the Hebrew Bible in terms of their witness to the good news and its christological fulfilment. This principle of selection was at work in the acceptance of that moral law in the Old Testament which is in continuity with the teaching and meaning of Jesus Christ, in the transformation and perfecting of other Old Testament moral mandates in the light of Jesus Christ, and in the rejection of certain other Old Testament regulations (for example, ceremonial laws) in the light of the new christological standard.

It is not adequate to view the Old Testament as though it were a flat surface: we must recognize its peaks and valleys. Because this is so, neither every moral injunction or practice nor every judgment about the nature of God in the Old Testament receives the status of divine revelation. Indeed, the Religious Right observes this principle of selection, for it does not defend slavery, concubinage, polygamy, or similar culture-bound practices. But its understanding of plenary verbal inspiration of Scripture and its own moral predispositions lead it to accept uncritically many of the views and practices of ancient Israel. The eye-for-an-eye ethic (set aside by Christ's own teaching) persists in many of its attitudes, ranging from criminal justice to war making. The acerbity and extremity of its attitudes toward sexual sins reflect the harshness found in early stages of moral sensibility in contrast to the tone and relationship embodied in Christ's own ministry.[7]

The Old Testament theme of the holiness of God, which underlies the moral judgments of the Religious Right, is a controlling factor in its doctrine of God. Preoccupied with this accent, it overlooks companion themes about the divine mercy and compassion, which are in fact found in the Old Testament and are elaborated in the New Testament on the basis of the life, death, and resurrection of Jesus Christ. Thus it misses the implications of these latter themes for one's attitude toward forms of human conduct which diverge from one's own.

A full assessment of the apocalyptic framework in which the Religious Right sets the destiny of Israel must await our review of eschatology. Here we note that its formal theological interest in the Jews is qualified by that very scenario. That is, Israel and its people today are seen as pieces on the chessboard of apocalyptic history, rather than as a nation or persons in their own right. As instrumental to the end-time design which the Religious Right perceives, they are affirmed conditional to their role in those purposes.[8] Obviously, to be seen as a pawn in a cosmic game is not to be understood for who one truly is or what one truly does. This instrumental view of the Jews may account for the anomaly of anti-Semitism among some of those very persons who profess a special theological interest in Israel.[9] It also may be responsible for a blurred political vision which responds to actions taken by or affecting the state of Israel according to an apocalyptic overlay rather than according to empirical facts and responsible judgment.

Perhaps the greatest departure from Christian doctrine by the Religious Right is its transfer of the status of special covenant from the elect of God in the particular history of Israel to another people. The functional elevation of America to the place of a chosen nation adds to the Christian story a chapter which is not in the Book. As we have observed, the United States shares with all peoples the universal covenants of Adam and Noah, and a status and role in the order of preservation. The historical influence exerted on it by the biblical visions of liberty and justice for all under God do make it accountable to these special professions of piety. But there is only one covenant stream in the Christian narrative through which God does the special work of redemption.

The confusion of a secular state with this special election does untold mischief. It feeds the flames of nationalism while at the same time dampening internal criticism. It encourages a swashbuckling military posture and incites foreign policy adventurism. The absence of the sense of prophetic judgment on the nation and the apostolic understanding of human nature shows up in superpatriotism and self-righteous fury.[10]

Ironically, the explicit teaching about Israel, conjoined to the displacement of Israel from its unique status by nationalist usurpation, represents a clandestine secular humanism making its way into yet another chapter of the Christian story. Here the human constructs of a right-wing political philosophy are substituted for sound doctrine.

CHAPTER 7

Jesus Christ

The Christian story reaches its dramatic turning point in this chapter. In the events of Bethlehem, Galilee, Calvary, and Easter, a figure emerges who changes the course of the history of the dealings between God and the world. Who he was and what he did are the subjects of the doctrine of Jesus Christ, his "person" and his "work." We shall examine the teaching of the Religious Right on Christology as it manifests itself in teachings about the incarnation and the atonement.

THE PERSON OF CHRIST

The understanding of the person of Christ in classical Christianity asserts the humanity, deity, and unity of Jesus Christ. As formulated at the Council of Chalcedon in 451, and held by virtually all branches of the church, this teaching seeks to set forth biblical teachings about the embodiment of the eternal Logos—the word, intention, and purpose of God—the "incarnation."

This doctrine is set forth in distinction to some perennial confusions about Christ's singular dignity. On the one hand, the "docetists," ancient and modern, have overspiritualized Jesus, thus disconnecting him and the saving work of God from ordinary life, the world of things, matter, and time. In this context classical Christianity boldly asserts the humanity of the Son of God. The "Ebionites" and their heirs, attuned to the humanity of Jesus, fall into the opposite mistake, reducing him to this level and denying that we have a chapter of the Christian story in which "very God of very God" came to dwell in our midst to struggle and suffer for us and with us. In the face of this, Christian tradition has declared the very deity of Jesus Christ. Against those who try awkwardly to put the two realities together, either by fusing them into one or dividing them into two, comes the affirmation of the one person in two natures "without division, separation, confusion, or change."[1]

The Religious Right is insistent on its loyalty to the ancient formula of the orthodox doctrine of the person of Christ. But once again we must take note of its presuppositional teaching on this subject as well as its formally stated doctrine. We shall then notice how implicit and explicit teaching may diverge as well as converge.

Although the Religious Right does not normally draw direct connections between its doctrine of the incarnation and its political practice, an important one is to be noted. To affirm that God comes into our midst at incarnation is to believe that this earth is both fit for this habitation of the divine presence and hallowed by it. Energy expended in the sanctification of the created order thus constitutes fit stewardship from the perspective of incarnation faith. The political mission of the Religious Right is coherent with its doctrine about the person of Christ.[2]

Along with this consistency of theory and practice, however, we may note some other considerations. These appear in the Religious Right's preoccupation with the sins of the body and its apocalypticism. In both cases the affirmation that flesh and history are hospitable to the divine presence seems to have faded into the background. In its concentration on sexual misdeeds as the primary forms of human sin, the Religious Right allies itself with those earlier Christologies whose suspicion of the flesh prompted them to deny the physical reality of Jesus. And in placing an apocalyptic grid on historical events—seeing our troubled age as a mere prelude to that happy day when God will replace time by eternity—the Religious Right is in effect qualifying the reality and seriousness of the stuff of history which the incarnation validates.

ASSESSMENT

Yes. What the Religious Right explicitly teaches on the incarnation stands squarely in the Christian tradition. At a time when concerted attacks are made on this fundamental Christian doctrine, one must welcome such a forthright assertion of the singular enfleshment of God at Bethlehem.[3]

No. The suspicion of the body expressed in the Religious Right's catalog of human sins moves in the direction of docetism in Christology. Influenced by the gnostic derogation of the flesh, it denies in practice the full humanity of the incarnate Lord, and thus contradicts the formal allegiance to classical doctrine. The superhistorical tendencies of apocalypticism further erode the importance of this world and this time, thus strengthening the docetic impulses in the Christology of the Religious Right.

The doctrine of the incarnation also sheds light on the abortion issue. Since this connection has not been given attention by traditional theology, we cannot treat this as an insight of classical faith but rather as a footnote to the discussion, needing much further exploration.

Both Scripture and the corresponding liturgical life of the Christian church make the *birth* of Christ the focal point of God's incarnational entry upon the human stage. Yet it is also true that the conception of Jesus is a crucial moment in the drama of enfleshment in Scripture and tradition: "Conceived by the Holy Ghost, born of the Virgin Mary."

To believe in the conception of Christ by the Holy Spirit is to affirm that all human life, from that point of its pilgrimage on, is sanctified by the divine presence in our midst. As such, fetal life enjoys a dignity derived from the incarnational action. The Religious Right's concern that the fetus not be considered simply a tumor to be removed at will is coherent with this implication of the doctrine of the person of Christ.

Scripture and tradition, however, fix on the birth of Christ into the world of human interrelationship, the world in which the divine drama is being acted out, as the time of special celebration. Here the angels sing and the shepherds come. The holy nativity marks God's full entry into the Christian story. While some Christian calendars mark the day of conception, all accent the day of birth. Bethlehem is the paradigm of incarnation.

As the conception of Christ cannot be identified or confused with the nativity of Christ, so there is a difference (derived from this fact in Christian faith) between the conception of a fetus and the birth of a child. Fetal dignity is grounded in the sanctification of life from its conception by the incarnational origin. But the fetus in the womb cannot be confused with the child in the manger. This difference should be recognized in the debates on abortion.

THE WORK OF CHRIST

As with much traditional Protestant theology it is the atonement rather than the incarnation that is the center of interest and controversy. "To know Christ is to know his benefits." The incarnation exists for the atonement. Who Jesus Christ is, is the warrant for what Jesus Christ does.

Atonement is at-one-ment, the uniting of separated parties to God's purposes. For the Religious Right, standing in the tradition of Protestant orthodoxy, reconciliation is the bringing together of humanity and God, who have been alienated from each other by the sin of the former and the judgment of the latter. On the cross Jesus Christ satisfies the penalty for human guilt by taking the punishment due the race. The blood of Jesus cleanses from sin because, as God-man, his infinite dignity makes the offering of his death equivalent to our deserved retribution, and he participates in the finite reality on which the curse must fall. As his death satisfies the punishment for our disobedience, his life satisfies the requirements of the perfect obedience expected of us. In the words of the old hymn, he is "of sin the double cure," achieving the requirements of both pardon and power.

At the heart of this penal substitutionary view of the atonement is the holiness of God. In traditional textbook expression, the divine righteousness is a necessary property in deity. While God *may* be loving, he *must* be holy.[4] The penalty must be exacted and the obedience secured before the love of God toward fallen humanity can be put in motion. In the face of the fall, therefore, the qualities that define deity are those of a righteous ruler, a sentencing judge, wrathful father. The moral rigor, the punishment of the lawbreaker, and the righteous wrath which have come to be associated with the Religious Right are directly related to its explicit interpretation of the atonement and the conception of God that underlies it.

ASSESSMENT

Yes. It is not hard to find theories of the atonement which attenuate or eliminate the holiness of God. Richard Niebuhr's description of acculturated religion applies to much conventional piety: "A God without wrath brought men without sin into a kingdom without judgment through the ministrations of a Christ without a cross."[5] The Religious Right's stress on sin, wrath, and judgment is an important corrective to "sloppy *agape.*" God *is* holy, the race *is* fallen, a righteous deity *does* hold us accountable for our rebellion.

The atonement wrought on Calvary can be no less than a deed done to save us from sin and its consequences. The cross is central to the reconciling work of God in Jesus Christ, the Lamb of God who takes away the sins of the world. Divine punishment is rendered through the passion and death of Christ, and mercy conquers wrath. Through obedience in life as well as faithfulness in death, Christ works reconciliation. These themes are part and parcel of any full-orbed understanding of the atonement.

An important strength of this view is its emphasis on the "passive" and "active" obedience of Jesus. He lived for us and he died for us. Atonement is no abstraction going on in a transcendent realm; it is effected in the moil and toil of our world. The quality of direct relationship to a real person who did for us something we could not do for ourselves—the theme of such familiar hymns as "What a friend we have in Jesus"—contributes to the power of this penal view. It "preaches well."[6]

No. Does the sacrifice of the gentle Jesus then satisfy the holy God and appease the angry Father? Is this the meaning of the atonement? Something fundamental is missing here: Paul's ringing declaration that "God was *in* Christ reconciling the world . . ." (2 Cor. 5:19). Atonement is an action done *by* God not *to* God. Jesus Christ himself is the God-man, not simply a man down on earth doing a work for and to the demanding God up in heaven. The penal substitutionary view of the atonement as rendered by the Religious Right opens a chasm between the God of the Bible and the action on Calvary.

The gap between what God does and what Jesus does is understandable in the light of the attribute the Religious Right takes as central to God's being, moral holiness. God's role in the crucifixion is seen as exacting a punishment whose severity fits the crime of human sin. To be sure, acknowledgment is made of a secondary quality in deity. No one who professes loyalty to the texts of Scripture could ignore John 3:16: "God so loved the world that he sent his only begotten Son." But the secondary status of this is clear from its second-hand presence in the atoning work: God provides an innocent human substitute, Jesus of Nazareth, to pay the penalty for human guilt. What this kind of formulation ignores is that the Son of John 3:16 is the God-man of Christian teaching, the eternal Son of the Father who took our flesh. As such, Calvary is the love of God dealing *first-hand* with the wages of sin. The love of God therefore emerges in Christian faith as a first quality within deity, indissoluble with, rather than subservient to, divine holiness.

The mystery of the atonement is that it is very God who takes the punishment for our sins into the divine being through the human suffering and death of Jesus Christ. What is profound about God's love is that it suffers in our place the judgment of divine holiness. As Luther expressed it, the blessing overcomes the curse; the divine love absorbs the divine wrath. Herein lies the meaning of "equivalency" of punishment. The suffering of God in the person of Jesus Christ opens up the

69

sluice gates of the divine mercy. The pain of God in the Lamb of God takes away the sins of the world.[7]

To understand in this way the work of God in the work of Christ is to change the terms of relationship in day-to-day questions of politics and economics. In those arenas compassion takes its place alongside holiness. Along with the call to moral accountability comes a suffering with and mercy for the last and the least. The victory of divine suffering and vulnerability which is achieved and declared on the cross and in the resurrection—the power of powerlessness—means that the world's view of the power is brought into question. Confidence in the "mighty man" is shown up for what it is, the wisdom of this world. The machismo philosophy of the Religious Right is a worldly point of view, expressing a secular humanism which sets itself against "the weakness of God [which] is stronger than men" (1 Cor. 1:25).

The atonement theory of the Religious Right focuses on the work of Christ on Calvary. Although its theologically more articulate exponents speak about the active obedience of Christ in his life as well as the passive obedience of his suffering and death, the Galilean ministry does not bulk large in the preaching and teaching of the Religious Right. Christ's obedience prior to his passion is seen in terms of achieving the perfection required for the "perfect sacrifice," and is thus only instrumental to the real work done on the cross. But the long tradition of Christian teaching on the work of Christ does not ignore this "prophetic office" of Christ in Galilee, thus following the gospels, which extensively record his words and deeds before crucifixion. Hence a full doctrine of the atonement will make room for the texts and teaching of this "Jesus of history."

The work of Christ which is manifest in Jesus' day-to-day ministry is disclosure. The one who frees us from the bondage of sin and guilt on Calvary is the one who liberated us from error and untruth during his ministry in Galilee. He reveals who God is, who we are, what we must do, and what God does and will do. In his life, teaching, and healing, a vision of the being and rule of God takes form. In the kingdom which is both here and near, God's holiness and love shine forth. Jesus comes to preach "good news to the poor ... to proclaim release to the captives ... recovery of sight to the blind, to set at liberty those that are oppressed, to proclaim the acceptable year of the Lord" (Luke 4:18 – 19). In his attitude and behavior as well as his teaching, he embodies mercy for the sinner, justice for the oppressed, compassion for the neighbor in need, love for the enemy, obedience to the Father, and joy in the Lord. In his life as well as in his death we have to do not only with the human ministry, but with the eternal Son incarnate, the God-man in our midst.

The political, economic, and social posture of the believer must be oriented to the God who was in Christ on the Galilean pilgrimage. Are the poor, the prisoner, the blind, and the oppressed the focus of the programs of the Religious Right? Is justice emblazoned on its banners? Is compassion for the needy in the foreground of its mission? Is love of the enemy at the heart of its policies?[8]

Only God can judge whether these things are finally so. Moreover, there is no simple translation of the vision of the kingdom into political programs, as we shall see in the next chapter. And it must surely be granted that the pro-life concerns in politics and the social service concerns in local church ministries of the Religious Right do reflect concern for the least and the last. But it takes a mighty effort in casuistry to make a case that the pro-gun, pro – capital punishment, pro – nuclear weaponry, pro – American nationalism, anti – women's rights crusades of the Religious Right are an expression of the prophetic office of Jesus Christ. These positions are more influenced by the secular values of the New Right than loyalty to the atoning work wrought in the Galilean ministry.[9]

In his *Institutes of the Christian Religion* John Calvin gave shape to a conception of the work of Christ which has had widespread influence in Protestant theology and also has currency in Roman Catholic and Eastern Orthodox teaching: the doctrine of the threefold office of Christ. Jesus Christ is prophet, priest, and king, the unity and fulfilment of the three dominant leadership roles in the Old Testament. The priestly role comes to focus in the sacrifice made on Calvary, the prophetic role in

Jesus' preaching and teaching in Galilee, and the royal office in the resurrection, although each of these segments of Christ's career is manifest in all the offices. This encompassing view of the work of Christ corrects reductionist notions that limit the atonement to one or another of the offices of Christ.

To confess that Christ has assumed the royal office is to believe that "He's got the whole world in his hands." Jesus Christ rules right now by virtue of his resurrection and ascension. The world is not in the hands of the evil one or the powers and principalities that seek to thwart the divine will. To be sure, the rule of Christ is still hidden, for the empirical evidence shows evil rampant, innocence slaughtered, sin infesting every soul, death as our common lot. But the eye of faith, fixed on the Easter event, sees what the eye of sight cannot know: Satan has been dethroned and Christ is king. No ultimate harm can come to the purposes of God. What is now for faith will someday be for sight; what is now in principle will be in fact. With this assurance the believer does not feel that he or she must rout the demonic forces; they already have been sent fleeing. The believer confronts the conflict with evil in a serenity that cannot be destroyed by the worst historical evidence and a confidence that sustains and empowers in the face of the worst odds. The Easter believer does not think that the overthrow of Satan depends on the exertion of human piety or morality.

This spirit, theology, and atmosphere differ sharply from both the rhetoric and posture of the Religious Right. Its stern sense of opposition to the forces of evil is indeed faithful to the reality of a fallen world. But the Religious Right goes beyond this in its belief that Satan in fact rules. A call to battle is issued in the confidence that the faithful can smite the foe, now in the guise of secular humanism, and defeat him.

With this cosmology, we find ourselves again in the environment of Zoroastrianism and Manichean dualism. A drama is in fact unfolding, and a struggle is in progress. But classical faith has confidence in the *already* of victory, even though it awaits the *not yet* of its completion. Moving expression to this assurance is given in Milton's vivid portrayal of the imagery of the book of Revelation:

The Old Dragon under ground
In straiter limits bound,
    Not half so far casts his usurped sway,
And wroth to see his Kingdom fail,
Swinges the scaly horror of his folded tail.[10]

The sword of the royal Christ has inflicted that mortal wound. We do not need a "mighty man" to do it.

The atonement theology of the Religious Right stresses the priestly work of Christ. Along with the strengths of this go profound weaknesses which separate God from the work of Jesus and divine holiness from divine love. The work of Christ as prophet is at best muted, and the work of Christ as king is missing. At key points cultural themes and extra-Christian perceptions take the place of classical teaching.

CHAPTER 8

The Church

In the Christian story, the work of the Spirit succeeds the work of Christ. After Easter comes Pentecost. Tongues of fire descend from the light of the ascended Lord. On Pentecost the Holy Spirit brings to be the body of Christ on earth.[1] How is this Christian community understood in the teaching and practice of the Religious Right?

The Religious Right's doctrine of the church draws heavily on precedents from what is called the left wing of the Reformation. The church is a community of those gathered out of the world by the decision of faith for a holy life here and heaven in the hereafter. The wheat has been separated from the tares; the remnant of true believers remains. The church is the virgin, pure and undefiled.

The congregations of the Religious Right are fashioned to be an alternative society in a corrupt culture.[2] The Thomas Road Baptist Church founded by the Reverend Jerry Falwell is typical. The fervor of its religious life is evident on its weekly television program and in its revivalist practices, which have increased its membership to 18,000 people. This growth and vitality is reflected not only in the large membership of the church and its huge television audience, but also in the founding of a Christian academy and a college. The church demands "the total involvement" of its members.[3] It enforces a code of behavior that distinguishes its people by such things as prohibition against smoking, drinking, cursing, and sexual promiscuity. It sets standards of dress and hairstyle, child-rearing and family relationship, with the authority of the father and the submission of wife to husband being stressed. Coherent with its hierarchical views of family life, business and politics, there is also a "chain of command" within the congregation reaching to the pastor who is the undisputed head.[4]

The "sect-type" church—to use the term of the German scholar Ernst Troeltsch (1866 – 1923)—in the left-wing Reformation tradition distinguishes itself from its surroundings by the fervor of its faith and the rigor of its moral and spiritual disciplines. These features continue in the Religious Right, with one important addition. Not only is personal piety expected from the membership, but also political piety. At a minimum this means registration for voting, with pastors and congregations of the Religious Right carrying on active registration and get-out-the-vote campaigns. But the Religious Right's political piety is usually far more specific. It entails loyalty to the church and/or pastor's view on "Christian issues," the catalog of contemporary concerns we detailed in Chapter 1. Frequently it means support for political candidates who espouse acceptable positions on those issues. And it also regularly involves corporate action to support these positions and people by way of public rallies, letters-to-the-editor campaigns, boycotts, and demonstrations.

The concept of the church operative in the theory and practice of the Religious Right is a merging of the three varieties of sixteenth-century Anabaptist spirituality: evangelical, conventicular, and revolutionary. The fervent faith and evangelistic outreach of the Religious Right are related to early Anabaptists who saw their mission as conversion of sinners. Its withdrawal from the corruptions of the world and its creation of an alternative society are linked with Anabaptist conventicles, which can be still seen in contemporary Old Order Amish counterculture. The feature that distinguishes the Religious Right most significantly from other forms of pietism in our time is the continuation of the revolutionary impulse of the Anabaptists of the city of Münster and the figure of Thomas Münzer. Recourse to violence to bring in the kingdom has not characterized the Religious Right, as was the case with sixteenth-century activists;

rather, the apocalyptic zeal to prepare the way for the coming of the Lord expresses itself in political zealotry.

ASSESSMENT

Yes. The contribution of a left-wing Reformation sensibility to the ecumenical church continues in the emphasis of the Religious Right on the church as a "company of the committed." Whenever the institutional church has accommodated itself to its surroundings so as to lose its distinctiveness of faith and life, "sect-type" communities have arisen to challenge this Babylonian captivity. In every time and place the larger church and local congregations need visionaries to shake them into taking account of their ultimate commitments. From the various orders within the church of the Middle Ages to the renewal movements within and among today's ecclesiastical institutions, the larger community has sometimes had the wisdom to stay in relationship to Christian visionaries. Then they become "critics-in-residence,"[5] enriching the church and themselves by a mutual give and take.

The alternative is to let the visionaries slip away into sectarianism, to the impoverishment of all parties. But even when such withdrawal happens, the church ecumenical and catholic can learn from its separatists. They invariably draw attention to the unattended issues and lackluster performance of institutional Christianity. There is not a little to be learned from the Religious Right. It teaches the spirit of dedication, reminds us of the mandate to offer a critique of contemporary culture, upholds the concern to strengthen marriage and the family, issues the call to social action, and helps show a way to employ modern technology in the mission of the church. The failure of organized Christianity in many of these areas has prepared the ground for the seeds the Religious Right has sown—as well as the weeds it has grown!

No. Plaguing the sect-type church is the occupational hazard of all visionaries—self-righteous fury. "Thank God I'm not like others!" is the cardinal sin of spiritual pride. To limit the church to—and define it as—the spiritually and morally pure is to separate the wheat from the tares by our hand in this time instead of by God's hand in God's time. "Let both grow together until the harvest . . ." (Matt. 13:30). The church, the community of forgiven sinners not self-proclaimed saints, is most itself when it lives under both the lure of its visions and the judgment of its dreams.

Two features of the current Religious Right aggravate the dangers of the sect spirit. One is its characteristic (although not exclusive) form as "independent churches," and in the video church as "independent preachers," relating responsibly to no larger Christian community than that of its own making.[6] Having chosen to cut off all meaningful bonds with their brothers and sisters in Christ, such religious entities easily fall prey to the influence—and whims—of "charismatic" personalities. Worse, they have no living connection with the wellsprings of the Christian tradition which can nurture them as a body in the growth of sound doctrine and life. The evidence of idiosyncratic and acculturated teaching throughout our study of the theology of the Religious Right is directly related to its separatist existence.

A second characteristic that compounds the problem of sectarianism in the Religious Right is the identification of highly specific political judgments with the boundary lines of church membership.[7] Who is in and who is out are determined by subscription to the list of political opinions and actions detailed earlier. Thus the marks of piety are the marks of political piety, which is to say, human judgments in the ambiguous arena of politics. This is a confusion of the church's perennial norms with partisan human opinion. Moreover, when a cause is denominated a "Christian cause," requiring the allegiance and unqualified endorsement of the church as such, the gospel becomes confused with transient, errant human opinion.

Wherever a secular humanism of the right intrudes its judgment into the church's proclamation and pedagogy, a forceful No must be uttered. The church is called to listen to the one word, Jesus Christ, and to proclaim that word alone, not to elevate the fallible words of human beings to the status of Christian proclamation and mission.

The admixture of the Word with human words plagues all Christians who attempt to relate their faith to political, social, and economic matters. It is a temptation for politically centrist Christians as well as the Christian right or left. Nevertheless, some wisdom about political implication and application, hard won in the struggles of the ecumenical church in the twentieth century, may be useful to repeat in this context:

(1) The concept of "middle axiom" represents a consensus that develops within the Christian community, and sometimes in the larger human community, about the translation of an overarching ethical norm (justice or freedom, for example) into the issues that come to the fore in a particular era. A *middle* axiom is one which does not specify the concrete application of the principle to a person, party, or program, but does scale down the more abstract norms to the ethos in which specific judgments are to be made. For instance, justice for black citizens in housing, jobs, public accommodations, voting, and education became an important middle axiom in the civil rights struggle. Justice for women, for the "elders" in our society, for the disabled and handicapped, and in areas of need and oppression is currently to the fore. A middle axiom as such does not have the weight of biblical authority and cannot therefore be identified with the church's proclamation. On the other hand, as a corporate judgment of the Christian community expressed in its councils of decision-making, it serves as a guideline for moral choices.

In its separatism, the Religious Right has denied itself what has been learned from this process. The result is that it makes immodest claims for its partial perspectives. Furthermore, its own position on a range of current issues runs exactly counter to the received tradition of corporate ecclesial thought.[8] Schism takes its toll in polity, theology, and morality.

(2) In an admittedly stumbling way, Christians involved in mainstream and ecumenical social action programs have learned to structure social witness in ways that maintain their integrity and force without confusing a particular action or pro-

gram undertaken by a sub-community within the church with the boundaries of church membership itself. Thus a "task force" within a congregation or larger ecclesiastical body may be set apart by the whole community to attend to a particular issue. It seeks to enlighten the larger group about the issue and to act on it in its own right. As such it does not speak *for* the church as a whole, but it speaks *to* it and acts *out* of it as a segment *in* it. Similarly, resolutions made in church councils speak *to* the constituency and not *for* it, even as they speak to a wider audience with the authority alone of their evidence and visions.

(3) In addition to these corporate ways of witness, ecumenical Christians are moving more and more in the direction of empowering their membership on site within the social, economic, and political worlds as the "ministry of the laity." Here the church in its corporate and collegial reality takes form in support groups, commissioning, training, accountability, and spiritual discipline.[9]

The Religious Right could profit from these structural lessons to avoid mistaking the boundaries of political allegiance with those of the church, with all the fragmentation and internal dissension that sooner or later comes in the wake of such wrongly drawn lines.

A final critique of the ecclesial pattern of the Religious Right has to do with the "chain of command" that prevails in many of its congregations. The vesting of nearly absolute power in the person and office of the pastor is as wrong within the church as it is in the world of the industrial baron and political autocrat. The "mighty man" philosophy, with its attendant suspicion of "democracy,"[10] does not comport with the awareness in the entire Reformation tradition of the temptations of power, nor, in particular with the opposition in the left-wing Reformation tradition, to bishop and king, and its commitment to the dispersion of power.

In this latter tradition, the Spirit is believed to be spread throughout the membership of the whole body, giving a variety of gifts rather than being concentrated in the person of the pastor. The horror of Jonestown and the People's Temple ought to warn our generation with a clarity seldom granted in history of the fatal dangers of pyramiding power in the pastoral office.[11] Sound doctrine about the fact of human sin, which manifests itself most virulently in spiritual pride, should alert us beforehand to the vulnerability of church institutions and leadership to these dangers.

CHAPTER 9
Salvation

The doctrine of salvation in a narrative presentation of Christian faith centers on what is sometimes called subjective soteriology—the application of the benefits of salvation wrought in the work of Christ (objective soteriology). How and what does the Holy Spirit work in those called to belong to him? Since society, as well as individuals, belongs to the risen and reigning Lord, the doctrine of salvation sequel to the work of Christ also gives attention to the deliverance from social evil in society and history. How is historical providence viewed after the work of Christ?

In the doctrine of personal salvation, the teaching and practice of the Religious Right loyally follow the order of salvation (*ordo salutis*) of Protestant orthodoxy: calling, regeneration, conversion (repentance and faith), justification, sanctification, perserverance, and glorification. An individual, called by God to be among the saved, is born again. He or she experiences that new being in personal repentance and faith, stands pardoned before God, grows in personal holiness, avoids the temptations of backsliding, and receives the blessings of heaven in the world to come. The entire pilgrimage is carried out by God's grace, not by human works.

The Religious Right gives a special turn to some of these phases in the journey of personal salvation. Authentic conversion is seen as revolutionary not evolutionary, a repentance and faith that takes hold in an instantaneous and dramatic way, often in a revival setting. As with many other born-again Christians, regeneration is seen as the intense personal experience given as a sign of one's new relationship to God, and not merely a status conferred in the waters of baptism.[1]

Sanctification, as in some other Protestant traditions, takes a decidedly perfectionist direction in the Religious Right. The claims made for the true believer in its operational theology, the absence of confession of sin in its liturgies, and its explicit teaching and preaching point to the assumption that sin does not persist in the life of true holiness.

The marks of the state of sanctification are indications of devotion to the political commitments of the Religious Right. While not all of the Moral Majority, as we have seen, are the redeemed of the Lord—since membership is open to moral citizens who respond to general revelation—it would be difficult to conceive of a saved soul who (unless for reasons of ignorance) opposed any of the items on the political agenda of the Religious Right. To be born of God is to be for the causes of God, and this understanding of sanctification takes very specific shape as it is lived out by Christians in America today. The personal holiness which evangelical piety expects of everyone is to be supplemented by a social holiness whose content is determined by the philosophies and programs of the political Right.

This politicization of salvation has repercussions in another aspect of the doctrine of the application of Christ's benefits. In contrast again to much of traditional born-again piety, the concept of salvation is broadened beyond the self to the wider society. It is not uncommon for proponents of the Religious Right to use the language of redemption for nations and their affairs.[2] The goal of the Religious Right is to save the United States—or, more exactly, to pray and work for God so that he might save it—from internal decadence and the external threat of Communism. God is at work in the world of social, economic, and political institutions, not only in a general providential way, but in a specific saving fashion—delivering us from the evils of secular humanism, saving the family, preserving the economic order, building up the state. Since much of this soteriological framework is placed in an eschatological setting, we shall deal with it further under the doctrine of consummation.

ASSESSMENT

Yes. The gift of evangelical piety and its *ordo salutis* is in its personal appropriation of the faith journey. This is a strength which the Religious Right shares. Salvation is seen as the deliverance of a person from sin and guilt. Here the dynamics of that journey out of darkness into light are explored. Here faith is rightly understood as a crucial decision, not something casually assumed, a new birth and not a new set of clothes. Here grace is lifted up as the pardon and power which makes the journey of faith possible.

To see that sanctification includes political vocation is another insight of the Religious Right. Piety cannot be confined to the personal virtues and disciplines; it spills out into the public arena. Salvation is world-historical as well as personal in the biblical story. The ascended Lord rules the nations as well as persons. Christ's liberating and reconciling work goes on in the midst of economic, political, and social bondage and alienation.[3] By its effort to relate itself to the redemptive activity it sees on the larger landscape of human history, the Religious Right challenges the restriction of the doctrine of salvation to interiority.

No. Along with the strengths of evangelical piety, however, some of its weaknesses come into the Religious Right's doctrine of salvation; and its special context accentuates these weaknesses to the point that their expression becomes destructive. In discussing the fall we referred to the theological and spiritual hazards of not taking human sin seriously enough. We return to that theme here.

The pilgrimage of faith pointed to in the *ordo salutis* is one with a real turning point in regeneration, conversion, and justification.[4] Sanctification is a stage of real growth and perseverance in holiness. But the about-face of repentance and faith is a beginning not an ending. The walk in the light from that point on is harassed at every step by darkness within and without. A fixation on the birth trauma ignores the growing up into adulthood which lies before the newborn. Soteriology is not eschatology: we are not yet what we shall be. Simplistic distinctions between "we" and "they" are thus not valid. This dichotomy recurs in the interpretation of sanctification. The perfectionist impulse obscures the sin that persists in the life of the redeemed, a sin whose dangers increase rather than decrease as its temptations ascend along the line of growth in holiness. There must be a place for continuing penitence alongside perseverance in the order of personal salvation, as is recognized in ancient Christian liturgy and piety.

When the principle of self-criticism provided by penitence is missing in a soteriology that merges personal and political piety, the results are predictable. Political positions and their exponents come to stand above criticism, since they are seen as sharing in the perfection attributed to the untainted state of sanctification. Gone is any sense of the ambiguity that attends human judgment. Finite opinions are elevated to infinite value. Secular humanistic political views come in the back door of the doctrine of salvation. Once again worldly notions are fused with ancient religious passions in the spirit of Zoroastrian dualism.

The positive aspect of the Religious Right's larger view of salvation—seeing the divine deliverance and healing in history—is joined to this negative element. Just as personal sanctification is too easily identified with elect individuals who espouse the correct political views, so social sanctification comes to be attributed to select nations and movements of social change. Superpatriotism, uncritical loyalty to the single issue positions we have mentioned and religious endorsement of them, "Christian politicians," and the effort to speak with a monolithic "Christian voice" on social and economic issues all demonstrate the same absence of self-criticism, and thus the penitence, that is missing in the perfectionism of personal salvation. A close scrutiny of the operating norm for judgments about where Christ is present in the affairs of nations shows more resemblance to the secular political line of the New Right than to Luke 1 or Matthew 25. No simple identification may be made between Jesus Christ and the secular movements of deliverance from poverty, hunger, and bondage, but he has taught us that he is present among those who minister to "the least of these" (Matt. 25:31 – 36).

Although confined to only one segment of the Religious Right—in particular, to some of the representatives of the video church—the presence of another concept of salvation should be noted here. This is evident in the commercialism of electronic religion. A "give to get" motif runs through the appeals of many television preachers. God's grace is tied implicitly— and sometimes explicitly—to offers made over the air and the financial support sought from the listener. The same sales pitch sometimes appears in the computerized mailings of the Religious Right. These overtures are strongly reminiscent of the selling of indulgences in the sixteenth century, which was instrumental in motivating Luther's protest. Salvation is by grace through faith. It cannot be bought. One cannot give in order to get. The Religious Right's contemporary flirtation with salvation by works is an act of faithlessness to its own Reformation heritage and another example of the intrusion of worldliness into its professions of Christian piety.

This *quid pro quo* philosophy is related to another practice of the electronic church which has implications for the doctrine of salvation. Televangelists have to keep their message simple. The constraints of time and the video medium are not conducive to investigating complexity.[5] Thus the style of the television commercial shapes the way the Christian message is given articulation. Slogans and quick-fix promises tend to replace the richness and subtlety of Christian faith and detour around the arduous road of the pilgrim's progress. Moreover, the success of glamour in secular television leads the "video vicars" to incorporate the same splash and flamboyance in their own methods of communication. The technical equipment and staging needed to do this requires great sums of money, so that the prime-time preacher takes on the habits and thinking of the secular entrepreneur.[6]

In this way the values of secular society provide the instruments of communication for the electronic church and thus make their way into the image of the Christian faith which it projects. We must ask whether the simplifications, worldliness, and entrepreneurial mentality of secular culture do not finally obscure the truth of salvation and its source in the Savior who "had no form or comeliness that we should look at him, and no beauty that we should desire him ... despised and rejected ... a man of sorrows, and acquainted with grief" who was "wounded for our transgressions ... , bruised for our iniquities" (Isa. 53:2, 3, 5).

CHAPTER **10**

Consummation

The doctrine of the end receives more attention from the Religious Right than most other Christian teachings. Why so? Does the sharp dualism we have noted throughout this theology discover a kindred spirituality in the apocalypticism of Daniel and Revelation? Some scholars argue that the influence of dualistic Zoroastrianism was in fact manifest in strands of post-exilic Judaism.[1] Does fear of the future drive some to the refuge of traditional values and lead them to paint the future in lurid colors and catastrophic shapes? Again, a good deal of evidence exists to show that times of historical peril or seismic change bring with them spiritual scenarios of proportionate dimensions.

However, Christian theological analysis cannot settle its case with psychological or sociological data, as valuable as they are. To dismiss a theological point of view because of its apparent nontheological origins is to fall victim to the "genetic fallacy." Our task here is to listen to and assess the truth claims of our sisters and brothers, acknowledging on the one hand that none of us is exempt from influence of forces lying beneath the surface of theology and on the other hand that God can raise up children of Abraham from stones. Theological truth may come from the commonest of origins.

"I am separatist, premillennialist, pretribulationist; . . . this is the terminal generation before Jesus comes."[2] Here in a nutshell is the view of the end with which we have to do in the Religious Right. But these code words need some translation.

APOCALYPTIC

Apocalypticism, or apocalyptic, is a species of the genus eschatology. Derived from the Greek word for "last things," eschatology is the traditional term for Christian teaching about the end, in the sense of both purpose (*telos*) and conclusion (*finis*). As it has been thought through in the theological tradition of classical Christianity, eschatology fixes on four great motifs, which appear in both the Apostles' Creed and the Nicene Creed: the resurrection of the dead, the return of Christ, the final judgment, and everlasting life in all of its richness of personal, social, and cosmic fulfilment.[3] Eschatology answers the questions of *what* the end is and *why* it is so as the fulfilment of the divine promises.

Apocalyptic, as it has appeared from time to time in the history of Christianity and in other religious traditions, is not satisfied with the ultimate what and why, but presses for more detailed answers. It wants to know where, when, how, and who. Not content to see through a glass darkly, it seeks for transparency, and this need is only requited by big, bold, and sharply defined technicolor images of the end.

To describe this quest for clarity with other images, we may say that apocalyptic supplies a *timetable, map, blueprint*, and *playbill* of the end. The timetable is a schedule of arrival and departures, all of them printed up for *this* season ("This is the terminal generation . . ."), thus answering *when*. The map furnishes the location of things to come. Jerry Falwell appears on one program about the Middle East pointing to Armageddon, where the final conflict will take place, indicating that it is 200 miles long, that 400 million people will be killed here, and the like. Thus, an answer is given to the question of *where*. The blueprint is a specification of the climactic events that are abuilding, the structure and character of things to come, thus answering *how*. Finally, we know the cast of characters because we are furnished with a playbill. The Antichrist, the angels, the saints, the beast of Revelation 13 are all identified. Thus we are told *who* will be involved.

In all these descriptions of things to come, there are sharp juxtapositions, stark and violent contrasts, no pale hues but all brilliant colors. The warlike imagery is heightened and the difference between the contestants is intensified. The forces of light and darkness are ranged against each other with absolute polarity, prepared for the final conflict.

Apocalyptic not only answers specific questions about the future but moves the place, time, characters, and trajectory of the end into the present.[4] The immediacy of the end means not only that things are soon to happen, but that they have already begun to happen. The curtain is now rising on the last act. We know this to be so because the signs are for the eyes of faith to see. But not only for the eyes of faith, for anyone who watches Pat Robertson at his globe describing events in the Middle East or who reads the complex interpretations of news items made by contemporary seers is enlightened. All the forecasting tools—timetable, blueprint, map, and playbill—are readily usable, enabling us to make sense of the phantasmagoria of apparently random events which seem so ominous for those who do not have the key to their meaning.

An example of this claim to making current events intelligible is the apocalyptic interest in Israel. The return of the Jews to their homeland, the establishment of the state of Israel, the conversion here and there of some Jews to Christianity, the challenge to Israel by Marxist countries and movements, Israel's 1981 bombing of the Iraqi nuclear reactor—all these events can be interpreted in the framework of apocalyptic scenarios.

There is a powerful attraction to the prognostications and interpretations of apocalyptic. We are given a real preview of coming events. Moreover, we have foresight, a clear run-through ahead of time of the Cecil B. DeMille—like production that is coming. Where the world is blind we see; where the world is ignorant we know. Thus the dualism we have noticed throughout the theology of the Religious Right is further strengthened by the promise of becoming a seer and a knower, living with secrets amidst the ignorant.

CONTEMPORARY APOCALYPTIC

If the preceding elements constitute the frame of apocalyptic, what is the big picture itself? In the foreground are the places and people of "pre-tribulation." Signs of the end are seen in the ubiquitous signature of secular humanism, in the world without God, in the amorality to which we have been introduced in other doctrines. What qualifies as evidence for decadence varies according to the era in which the apocalypticist lives. Earlier seers generally cited Communism, fluoridation of water, and the founding of the United Nations (1950s); before that it may have been biblical criticism or the modernist heresy (1920s). These themes persist among some in the Religious Right. But today it is chiefly the secular humanist who is seen as used by Satan to promote homosexuality, abortion, divorce, adultery, pornography, the breakdown of family life, the erosion of liberties, governmental tyranny, military weakness, the corruption of public education, and the spread of Marxism.

The presence and power of secular humanism are seen as prelude to the more specific scenarios of Scripture. Soon the Antichrist will begin his work in the midst of the apostate churches, while the beast will rise in the political arena. Together they will unleash three-and-a-half years of misery. Meanwhile events in Israel have been unfolding in pre-tribulationary patterns—the return to the homeland, the formation of the Jewish state in 1948, the success of movements like "Jews for Jesus" in converting some Jews to Christianity, and the Soviet threat to Israel. All this is seen as taking place on the eve of the tribulation itself.

The beginning of the great time of troubles will be marked—on the pre-tribulationist viewpoint—by the rapture. Jesus will come for his church and meet them halfway, literally in the air, taking them to the safety of the heavenly ramparts. Then the tribulation begins. Antichrist will be revealed, two prophets will appear in Jerusalem, 144,000 Jewish witnesses will be sealed to serve, ten nations will give their authority to Antichrist, and the beast-king will guarantee Israel's security for seven years. World

War III will begin as Russia and the Arabs attack Israel and the Western powers, eventuating in a nuclear holocaust.

Then come the two trumpets of judgment and the beginning of the middle of the tribulation. The believers who were not raptured earlier are now brought to be with Christ. Satan is cast out of heaven and indwells the slain body of Antichrist. Satan slays all the saints still left, the 144,000 Jewish witnesses. He indwells the beast and slays the two prophets in Jerusalem. The slain prophets are resurrected and translated. Other events of a similar nature unfold.

The time of tribulation comes to a close with the return of Christ and his saints for the final confrontation of Armageddon. Satan is cast into the bottomless pit, and the beast and false prophets are hurled into the lake of fire. The throne of Christ's judgment is then established, and Christ rules on the earth for a thousand years of peace and harmony. The goats who followed Antichrist have proceeded into the lake of fire, and the sheep who believed and befriended the saints of the tribulation enter into the millennium and repopulate the earth. At the end of the millennium, Satan is released for a little season, and a last insurrection takes place. This, however, is quelled, and Satan is sent permanently to the lake of fire. The great throne of judgment is established, and all unbelievers are sent also to the lake of fire. The present earth and heaven are destroyed, the new Jerusalem descends on the earth, and a new heaven and earth come to be where all believers dwell in blessedness with Christ for eternity.

ASSESSMENT

Yes. In its apocalyptic the Religious Right surely cannot be accused of disloyalty to the narrative character of Christian faith. This is high drama. As in every good story, there is resolution of conflict and grand climax. Here, too, the movements of history are taken with high seriousness, and the activity of God is perceived in the passage of events, driving toward a victorious culmination. The action is "out there" in history, not "down there" in the interiors of the spirit or "up there" in a world beyond divorced from the moil and toil of earth—as is often the case in the pietisms and transcendentalisms of other religions or ahistorical forms of Christianity.

Furthermore, in a day and age when secularism offers its own eschatology in competition with Christian faith, we find in this apocalyptic a firmly theocentric vision of the future challenge to that anthropocentric one. Secular scenarios range from the optimistic (though usually chastened these days) views of Western modernity, certain that a trustworthy human nature aided by high technology will remake creation, through the confidence of Marxist millenarianism that the dialectic of history will resolve the contradictions of oppressor and oppressed, that the proletariat will triumph and usher in the end of a classless society, to the nightmare scenarios of the extinction of the race by its own hand through nuclear holocaust or ecological disaster. Falwell and Robertson are unwilling to let these secular prognostications go unchallenged by the Christian community. History is not in the hands of human contrivance or historical determinism, fate or chance; it is the theater of God's own glory. So they provide another script.

Again, this eschatology does not call its adherents away from history but girds them for battle in it. Instead of retreating from the world, the Religious Right spiritedly comes to grips with it and its issues. Apocalyptic—at least this form of it— empowers. And the historical action is intensely political. The way is prepared for the Lord by making the environment hospitable for him via the ballot box, over the air waves, through the halls of commerce, in the homes of the land. Here is a "theology of hope" which takes its cue from the vision ahead, challenges the status quo in the light of it, and seeks to set up signposts along the historical routes to the coming kingdom. The escapism and narcissism of many secular and religious movements of the day are challenged by a vigorous and urgent call to enter into historical action.

Finally, within the husk of apocalyptic is the kernel of classic Christian eschatology. We find here a confidence that the suffering Christ will be the triumphant Christ, that the vaporous spiritualism of too much Christianity is to be rejected in favor of the full-blooded prospect of the resurrection of the body, that the rebellious human race is accountable for its sin and subject to divine punishment, and that the fulfilment of God's future is social and cosmic in scope not the individualistic pie-in-the-sky of the mystical cognoscenti whose works clutter the paperback racks.

No. The Christian faith is indeed high drama. The Religious Right capitalizes on this in its detailed apocalyptic. The story, we have insisted, is chronicled for us in the storybook, and the Religious Right directs us to that charter for its own narration. The question we must ask is: Just what is the conclusion, according to that book?

For the answer we return to our earlier discussion of authority. As we saw there, the classical principle for interpreting Scripture directs us to the christological and gospel norms and to the resource and setting which help us make our way into the source and its center. That method fixes our attention on the enduring eschatological motifs of biblical faith rather than the transient metaphors of apocalyptic.

The wisdom of the great tradition of Christian thought about the end, as it is found in the creeds and catechisms of classical faith, has always been distinctly reserved about the where, when, how, and who questions. Though affirming no less boldly the resurrection of the dead, the return of Christ, the final judgment, and everlasting life in its personal, social, and natural dimensions, it has declined to furnish a timetable, map, blueprint, or playbill. From the second-century Montanists, who forecast an imminent end in great detail, through the millennialist excitement at the year 1000, to the numerous movements whose discredited prophesies of the date of the end litter the nineteenth and twentieth centuries, catholic faith has remained content to affirm the macrocosmic verities while making no claims about the microcosmic details of time and place, process and personnel.

This prophetic modesty is rooted in the testimony of Scripture itself: the source confirms the resource. Scripture as a whole, considered in terms of its great refrains, its recurring affirmations about the not yet, returns time and again to the four traditional eschatological motifs. That the story comes to a victorious end and in what that end consists with regard to the future of Christ, the future of the rebel human race, the future of the implacable love of God, and the destiny of the whole creation—these are the essentials of the tale, integral to its telling, answering the why and wherefore questions. The christological and evangelical norms—Christ and the gospel story—establish amidst the excitement and testimony of the early years of the apostolic community that which lasts as doctrine, "the dogma within the kerygma."[5]

The apocalyptic texts and themes in Scripture are random utterances, in sharp contrast to the eschatological regularities. For example, the elaborate doctrine of a thousand-year reign of peace is based on only one passage in the whole Scripture, nine verses in the twentieth chapter of Revelation, the most figurative of the Bible books. A fundamental Christian teaching about eschatology cannot be built on so narrow a textual base, through and through metaphorical, any more than a fundamental teaching about ministry can be constructed on the single exchange, similarly shot through with metaphor, recorded in Matthew's gospel: "You are Peter, and on this rock I will build my church" (Matt. 16:18). Moreover, the use of the best instrument of reason within the Christian community—our third and second concentric rings of authority—in the form of careful biblical scholarship demonstrates that many of the texts appealed to in apocalyptic have highly specific first-century referents, and cannot be torn out of their proper setting in order to argue fanciful modern hypotheses.

In telling the story, the Bible sticks to the storyline captured in the great refrains essential to the narrative, avoiding the temptation to say more than is required. This theological modesty is as much rooted in the character of the God portrayed as it is in the tale being told. Divine sovereignty does not sit comfortably with human pretensions to inside knowledge about God's future. The freedom of God is not in bondage to human speculations.

God indeed keeps the divine promises. The eschatological

trajectories rise out of the central act in the Christian drama: Christ will be triumphant, sin will be judged, faith will be vindicated, and the world will be transfigured. But how these things will be, where and when and who will be the *dramatis personae*, lie within the freedom of the divine will. We cannot penetrate the veil drawn across the final future. And because the end of history entails the transmutation of this world, and is thus in a dimension continuous with but beyond time, it is impossible to capture the events and movements of the end in the finite and broken language of this world. When the apocalyptic of the Religious Right attempts to identify events *in* history as eschatology, a form of secular forecasting is substituted for the eschatology of a transformed creation, which puts an end to the secular realm as such. Ironically, this secularization in eschatology is akin to the secularized humanisms, with their predictions of either heaven or hell in history, their forecasts of a millennial kingdom of peace and the end of class warfare or of an Armageddon-like nuclear or ecological disaster.

Nevertheless, even though the apocalyptic passages in Scripture raise and answer particular questions not essential to the Christian story, and even though their focus on colorful drama diverts attention from the classical eschatological visions, they did serve an important purpose for some first-century Christian communities. And they still have value for us today if, in Reinhold Niebuhr's words, they are taken "seriously though not literally." The symbols in the book of Revelation helped to buoy the faith of persecuted Christians both in the message of hope they conveyed in metaphors of apocalyptic judgment and redemption and in the particulars of the seer's code which identified enemy and friend.

Furthermore, such events as the millennium and such figures as the Antichrist have a perennial significance for faith and theology. The millennium, as the anticipation of a period of peace and justice in this world, is a reminder that the hope for historical evidence of the purposes of God is not an illegitimate expectation for the Christian, even though the perfections attributed to historical fulfilment by the apocalyptic mind must be drastically qualified by the persistence of sin. The millennial hope for history in the New Testament must be cast in the figures of foretaste, earnest, and firstfruits, thereby acknowledging its still fragmentary nature. This emerges in Revelation in the portrayal of a battle still to be waged after the millennium. The appearance of the Antichrist and the beast symbolize the persistence of evil at the end point of history, and therefore no simple escalator theory of progress is possible for Christians. Whatever growth of goodness takes place in history is imperiled by commensurate forces.

The foregoing has to do with the theological error of substituting apocalyptic for the eschatology set forth throughout the Christian tradition according to the christological and evangelical norms of Scripture. But there is mischief as well as mistake in the apocalyptic of the Religious Right. Its interpretation of current events and people can have disastrous consequences. Unlike the apolitical posture of traditional apocalypticism, which uses the forecast of catastrophe to draw its people apart from the world and prepare them for something done to and for them, the apocalyptic scenarios of the Religious Right are used to draw people into partisan action within the unfolding drama.

This changes the character of political involvement from the messy push and pull of compromise and conciliation in a pluralistic society to the clearcut polarization of the armies of righteousness and unrighteousness. Human political judgments shot through with finitude and sin are exempted from historical ambiguity by being transferred to an arena where evil and good are thought to be seen with total clarity. The volume of political rhetoric is raised to the level of thunderclaps of the end. One's political opponent becomes the Antichrist and the beast, which means that measures appropriate to the conflict of Armageddon can be legitimated by the legions of decency arrayed against the troops of the blasphemer.

Here again we see the covert entrance of Zoroastrian dualism into Christian proclamation. This perversion of Christian faith destroys political dialogue and rends the fabric of the common life. It breeds the arrogance and intolerance which mark many single-issue groups whose constituencies are members of the Religious Right. And it bodes ill for the future, as the apocalyptic drama unfolds and the maps and charts of true believers develop heightened expectations and encounters whose stakes are ever higher.

The concentration of apocalyptic in the Religious Right also downplays and distorts the teaching of faithful doctrine. The more attention given to the where, when, how, and who questions, the less is given to the why and wherefore affirmations of eschatological teaching. Confidence that Christ is truly Lord—a faith grounded in the resurrection and crowned by the Parousia—gives way to obsessive fears of Satan and tense and strenuous campaigns against demonic forces. Thus the final disposition of things turns out to be more and more in our hands. Again, the hope of final justice for the poor and oppressed in the kingdom and the judgment on the tyranny of the mighty, themes so central to the biblical picture of the end, are lost from view. With them disappears the empowerment in hope and action for the disenfranchised. And again, the striking eschatological hopes for a redeemed nature, "a new heaven and a new earth," and with it the ecological imperative, are lost on the apocalyptic Religious Right. Tacitly or openly, they endorse the destruction of the environment, unchallenged by Scripture and the traditional eschatology of the Christian community.

The end of the story indeed is coming in God's good time. Christian faith witnesses to that purpose and finality. It challenges all the illusions of secularized eschatology that the future is made or unmade by our human machinations. It calls into question views of the end in which secularism takes the form of an immoderate human curiosity and control and projects its apocalyptic scenarios onto contemporary history, thereby obscuring the mystery and majesty of biblical visions and losing the serenity of spirit appropriate to the not yet and the sobriety of political action befitting the now.

CHAPTER 11

God

The understanding of God grows out of the narrative of faith. Now that we have traced the Religious Right's conceptions of each chapter in the tale, their picture of the main figure takes form and substance. This corresponds with how the classical doctrine of God developed. The understanding of salvation provided a framework for the earliest formulations of the tri-unity of God, the "economic trinity" built up from the acts of creation, reconciliation, and redemption—Father, Son, and Spirit in their respective missions. Standing alone, this would be modalism, a heresy which does not do justice to the full God-ness of the three "Persons," or conceals an unknown fourth actor behind sequential masks as in the roles played in the ancient theater. The economic trinity keeps company, therefore, with an "immanent trinity," the eternal subsistence within the deity of all three persons.

As the doctrine of the trinity develops out of the saga of faith, so the traditional attributes of perfection receive their meaning from deeds done in history. What traditional theology calls the formal qualities of God—ommipotence, omniscience, omnipresence, eternity, infinity, and personality—are those of the one who defines what they mean by what is done in the divine biography. The same is true of the so-called material qualities, which pour content into the formal molds. While there are various ways of expressing these attributes, the two defining characteristics are *holiness* and *love*. God is utterly righteous in his glory and holds us accountable for our disobedience. Yet mysteriously joined to this majesty is a long-suffering compassion absorbing the consequences of sin and turning away the divine wrath by the divine mercy. Out of this profound drama in deity the Christian story itself is born.

The Christian Right is explicitly orthodox in its doctrine of God. Its commitment to the trinity, both economic and immanent, is firm. Its belief in the formal qualities of deity, particularly the divine omnipotence, is undoubted. It does not deny the paradoxical unity of holiness and love. But as in earlier teachings, here too there is a functional doctrine as well as a theoretical one. Out of the emphases in each chapter of the story another picture of the main actor in the drama begins to emerge.

The outstanding feature of this implicit doctrine of God is holiness. The name *Moral* Majority itself suggests the stress on a moral deity. God's righteousness is in the foreground at the beginning, center, and end of this version of the Christian narrative. God sets Adam and Eve in the Garden of Eden as probationers to test their obedience, and when they fail he condemns them and their heirs to the punishment due them. The focus of the next chapter of the story is the law laid down on Sinai and the breach of that law by the codes and practices of secular humanism. At the center of the Christian saga it is the punishment of the just Judge and the wrath of the angry Father which the atoning work of Jesus must deal with. In the doctrine of the church, the saving faith of the righteous remnant constitutes the body of Christ. In the Religious Right's call to a life of piety, holiness stands out. And in the last chapter of the story, all the emphasis falls on texts which portray the destiny of the damned and the saved, and the tradition of God's patient mercy (cf. Ezek. 18:32; 2 Pet. 3:9) is silenced. Furthermore, the dualism to which we have called attention throughout the narrative of the Religious Right—and in its sharpest form at the end—dovetails perfectly with the stress on God's holiness. Dualism *is* the contest between the God of righteousness and his armies of light and the forces of unrighteousness and night.

The doctrine of God of the Religious Right has its antecedents in one strand of Protestant orthodoxy. To put it in the language of technical theology, it views the essence of God as the divine holiness alone; God's love is, formally speaking, accidental. While God *may* be loving, God *must* be holy. God may or may not be merciful to sinners, but no such option exists when it comes to holiness—hence the constraint of the divine wrath. This notion functions throughout the doctrinal system of the Religious Right.

God in the classical Christian understanding of the story is *holy love*. Both holiness and love are integral to the divine essence.[1] Utterly righteous, God holds the world accountable for its rebellion against the divine purposes. We are the object of the divine wrath and the subject of the divine punishment. God is utterly loving and redeems the world in its rebellion against the divine purposes. Creation is the object of the divine mercy and the subject of the divine deliverance. There is no Christian story without these paradoxical assertions. Those who cannot live with the strain and pain of paradox relax the tension by eliminating one of the components. The Christian left dissolves the holiness and reserves the love, and the Christian right eliminates the love and trumpets the holiness.

This paradox cannot be explained, but it can be explored. In the believer's encounter with the gospel, the unity of holiness and love is demonstrated in experience and illumined by the Spirit. In that engagement of the soul with the atoning work of Christ on the cross, God's harshest judgment takes the form of quintessential love. We understand the depth of our own sin by the wound we have inflicted and the death we have brought to the Son of God. God's love pours the hot coals of its judgment on our heads. We understand that we *were* there when they crucified our Lord. Yet in the same confrontation we see the other side of the cross, the love that accepts the unacceptable and forgives the sinner. And we know that this is so because love has paid the price for us, absorbing the divine judgment, taking its full cost on Calvary. This is a paradox that invites the spirit into an ever deeper exploration, but into a mystery always unfathomable.

In the divine biography and in Christian autobiography, God is always holy love. Each of these qualities is essential.

Love begins the story, takes it to its centerpoint, and brings it to its close. But this kind of love cannot violate its holy essentiality, cannot be transformed into sentimental indulgence and cheap grace. It must satisfy the demands of righteousness. That is why the profoundest levels of the divine life are those of *suffering* love, the pain of God in Christ which purges sin, conquers evil, and overcomes death.

Out of this vulnerability the Christian way of life grows: the believer has been shown compassion and the forgiven sinner is able to forgive sinners. But this forgiveness is no more devoid of righteousness than is the model of holy love, a compassion and mercy joined to a passion for justice, a love of the sinner wrathful with the sin. The having and not having of Christian life short of the kingdom never achieves the perfection of the divine unity of holiness and love, but knows that this is what it is made for. Confessing that it misses the mark, it nevertheless always reorients itself to that vision.

As we have noted, the Religious Right leaves no doubt about the quality of rigorous righteousness in God. Its preaching—particularly its evangelical entreaties—speaks insistently about the love of Jesus. Its formal commitment to the biblical texts and to orthodox Christianity cannot help holding it to the love of God. But the Religious Right's testimony about the attributes of God in its construction of the Christian narrative leaves little room for redemptive love and therefore for the dialectic of wrath and mercy. The length to which God goes in creation and covenant to beckon the world toward its purposes, the wideness of God's mercy in the world, the firmness of the divine solidarity with us in the incarnation and atonement, the birth of a church for forgiven sinners, personal reconciliation by a gracious love received in faith, redemption in the world to come, the cosmic love which brings a new heaven and a new earth, and the unending love which pursues the last and the lost through eternity itself—these are decisive themes in the Christian faith. They are difficult to find in the narrative of the Religious Right.

Irony and contradiction are evident here too. The Religious Right strangely mutes its central theme of holiness at critical points. One looks in vain in the proclamations, policies, and political programs of the Religious Right for a prophetic denunciation of those who live at the pinnacles of power, a judgment found in both Old and New Testaments. The condemning to hell of the rich man who had feasted while Lazarus suffered, the rich who cannot squeeze through the needle's eye, David the king challenged by Nathan the prophet, Caesar confronted by Christ and the apostles, the economic and political principalities of this world on whom the wrath of God descends and for whom the just recompense of God will be meted out in this world and the next—all these biblical themes of divine righteousness are curiously absent from the theory and practice of the Religious Right. The secular humanism of the political right, with its legitimation of wealth, power, and privilege, has been smuggled into the gospel, and fundamental truths about God's holiness are filtered out.

The strangest lapse from Christian teaching about divine sovereignty occurs at the very heart of the Religious Right's practice. Especially the Reformed tradition—the stream of Protestantism to which most of the Religious Right belong—has proclaimed the sovereign freedom of God. This "Protestant principle" is ever on guard against attempts to bring God down from the heights of his glory or to identify human constructs and judgments with transcendence. Let God be God! Do not confuse the infinite majesty with finite and fallen opinions and systems of humankind. The divinization of human creation is idolatry, the vanity of Adam who sought and seeks still to seize the prerogatives of deity.

When the Religious Right unambiguously identifies its political causes and its specific policy judgments with God's cause and judgment, however, divine sovereignty is violated. When the inflated rhetoric of the Religious Right identifies a political opponent with Satan, the same confusion of transcendence and immanence is happening. In these confusions of historical phenomena and human creation with the warfare between God and the Evil One, we have the expression of a Zoroastrian theology and not the Christian story. The sovereign freedom of God cannot be in bondage to our opinions and projects. The universal sin which infects all these projects and the universal grace which can use an Assyrian rod and can make the wrath of the world praise God does not allow us to read and write history by a simplistic juxtaposition of our light and their night.

Conclusion

In a few years Christians will mark the fiftieth anniversary of the Barmen Declaration. In 1934 the Confessing Church in Germany gave unforgettable voice to its central allegiance. Confronted by a "German Christian" reinterpretation of the gospel, Barmen asserted:

> Jesus Christ, as he is attested for us in Holy Scripture, is the one Word of God which we have to hear and which we have to trust and obey in life and in death. We reject the false doctrine, as though the Church could and would have to acknowledge as a source of its proclamation, apart from and beside this one Word of God, still other events and powers, figures and truths, as God's revelation.[1]

These things must be said again a half century later in another land. No "blood and soil" philosophy or nationalist movement comparable to German Nazism imperils the United States right now, contrary to the inflated rhetoric of some critics of the right. But the perennial temptation of confusing God's word with one or another human word is very much with us in the Religious Right.

In this book I have tried to lay bare the theological presuppositions of the political and moral programs of the Religious Right. In every doctrinal area we have seen loyalty to important aspects of classical Christian conviction. At the same time, each of the chapters of the Christian story has told of basic distortions which warrant Senator Mark Hatfield's evangelical indictment:

As a Christian, there is no other part of the New Right ideology that concerns me more than its self-serving misuse of religious faith. What is at stake here is the very integrity of biblical truth. The New Right, in many cases, is doing nothing less than placing a heretical claim on Christian faith that distorts, confuses, and destroys the opportunity for a biblical understanding of Jesus Christ and of his gospel for millions of people.[2]

By examining a series of basic Christian beliefs we have seen that there is more than one kind of secular humanism to be reckoned with in our time. The substitution of human opinion for God's Word, Jesus Christ, can take place under the most pious of auspices. The implicit secular humanism of the Religious Right which imports partisan political judgments and culture-bound mores into the proclamation of the gospel, is as anthropocentric as the explicitly self-congratulatory humanisms of the secular left. The "perspective"[3] we have seen at work in many points of Christian doctrine—not all, by any means—rises out of one sector of contemporary secular experience, the politics and culture of the right. It is processed through a small, hospitable sector of ecclesial experience. Finally it takes charge of the purported biblical source and norm through a highly selective use and interpretation of texts. In many areas of Christian teaching this theological method arrives at conclusions that diverge from classical Christian teaching with its christological norm, inclusive biblical source, and full-orbed ecclesial resource.

The response to the Religious Right from within the Christian community must be a resolute commitment to its own fundamental framework of faith. As with Barmen, we must call ourselves and our brothers and sisters to attend to the one Word, Jesus Christ, and to tell our own tale, the Christian story, without addition or subtraction.

In the light of that Word we too shall make our political decisions. But that light illuminates the gift of Christian freedom. We are freed from the illusion that our frail judgments, whether on the right or left end of the political spectrum, can be identified with the Word of God. Christian liberty means that we are free of the ideologies of the right or left, and even free enough to say a human "Yes" or "No" or "Yes and No" to the passions and proposals of one or another when faith and facts warrant it. "For freedom Christ has set us free; stand fast therefore, and do not submit again to a yoke of slavery" (Gal. 5:1).

Notes

INTRODUCTION

1. "I believe the 1980s will be a decade of destiny. During the critical years of the 1980s it will be determined whether we continue to exist as a free people" (Jerry Falwell, *Listen, America!* [New York: Doubleday Publishing Co., 1980], p. 101). For Falwell's goals for the decade see his "Future-Word: An Agenda for the Eighties" in *The Fundamentalist Phenomenon: The Resurgence of Conservative Christianity* (Garden City: Doubleday & Co., 1981) , pp. 186 – 223. While the book's cover says only "edited by Jerry Falwell," the title page adds "with Ed Dobson and Ed Hindson." In the Foreword, Falwell indicates that he asked his two associates to write the book. Falwell himself has written the Foreword and the concluding chapter. This is an important, well-researched study, tailored of course to the ideological purposes of its sponsors.

2. Leaders of Moral Majority, Inc. insist that their own program is limited to four issues: "pro-life," "pro – traditional family," "pro-morality," and "pro-America." See Jerry Falwell, "My Turn: The Maligned Moral Majority," *Newsweek*, Sept. 21, 1981, p. 17. For reasons why some of the other items on a broader Religious Right agenda are not officially stressed see "An Interview with the Lone Ranger of American Fundamentalism," *Christianity Today*, Vol. XXV, No. 15 (Sept. 4, 1981), pp. 26 – 27.

3. Book-length efforts to diagnose, evaluate, or sketch out an alternative view include: Robert E. Webber, *The Moral Majority: Right or Wrong?* (Westchester, Ill.: Cornerstone Books, 1981); Erling Jorstad, *The Politics of Moralism: The New Christian Right in American Life* (Minneapolis: Augsburg Publishing House, 1981); Peggy L. Shriver, *The Bible Vote: Religion and the New Right* (New York: The Pilgrim Press, 1981); Jeffrey K. Hadden and Charles E. Swann, *Prime Time Preachers* (Reading, Mass.: Addison-Wesley Publishing Co., 1981); and Martin Marty, *The Public Church: Mainline-Evangelical-Catholic* (New York: The Crossroad Publishing Co., 1981). In *The Fear Brokers* (New York: The Pilgrim Press, 1979), Senator Thomas J. McIntyre with John C. Obert does an earlier analysis of the New Right indicating its association with the then-burgeoning Religious Right.

In *The Bible Vote* Peggy Shriver has assembled quotations from, documents of, and citations of many of the published responses of "Other Christian Voices and Moralities" (pp. 42 – 95, 103 – 150). We underscore here some of those and add a few more: "Christian Theological Observations on the Religious Right Movement," a statement by denominational executives (Oct. 21,

1980) reprinted in *The Bible Vote*, pp. 107 – 111; "A Pastoral Letter from the Bishops (Episcopal)" (Oct. 8, 1980), *ibid.*, pp. 111 – 115; "What's Wrong with Born-Again Politics: A Symposium," *The Christian Century*, Vol. XCVII No. 32 (Oct. 22, 1980), pp. 995 – 996, 1002 – 1004; "Can My Vote be Biblical?", a statement by Evangelicals for Social Action, *Christianity Today*, Vol. 24, No. 16 (Sept. 19, 1980), pp. 1035 – 1038, and Editorial, *ibid.*, p. 1032; "An Interview with the Lone Ranger of American Fundamentalism"; Tom Minnery, "The Man Behind the Mask: Bandit or Crusader"; Carl F. H. Henry, "The Fundamentalist Phenomenon: The Ricochet of Silver Bullets"; all articles in *Christianity Today* issue on "Unmasking Jerry Falwell and his Moral Majority," Vol. XXV, No. 15 (Sept. 4, 1981), pp. 1095 – 1104; Robert Zwier and Richard Smith, "Christian Politics and the New Right," *The Christian Century*, Vol. XCVII, No. 31 (Oct. 8, 1980), pp. 937 – 941; Robert McAfee Brown, "Listen, Jerry Falwell!", *Christianity and Crisis*, Vol. 40, No. 21 (Dec. 22, 1980), pp. 360 – 364; papers from Public Policy Conference, Board for Homeland Ministries, United Church of Christ (Dec. 4 – 5, 1980), especially those of Robert Sandon and James Nelson; papers from the Electronic Church Consultation University (Feb. 6 – 7, 1980); Erling Jorstad, "The New Christian Right," *Theology Today*, Vol. XXXVIII, No. 2 (July 1981), pp. 193 – 200; Marguerite Michaels, "Billy Graham: America is Not God's Kingdom," *Parade*, Feb. 1, 1981, pp. 6 – 7; a selected listing by Richard Pierard, "Bibliography on the New Christian Right," in *TSF Bulletin* (Nov./Dec. 1981), pp. s-1 – s-4.

    It has not been that long since the publication of criticisms of the earlier religious and secular "Radical Right." Those works continue to have relevance in the new setting. See especially Erling Jorstad, *The Politics of Doomsday: Fundamentalists of the Far Right* (Nashville: Abingdon Press. 1970); John H. Redekop, *The American Far Right: A Case Study of Billy James Hargis* (Grand Rapids: William B. Eerdmans Publishing Co., 1968); John Charles Cooper, *The Turn Right* (Philadelphia: The Westminster Press, 1970); The Anti-Defamation League, *Christian Friends: The Radical Right & Religion*, reprint from Vol. XXII, No. 3; Daniel Bell, ed., *The Radical Right* (Garden City: Doubleday & Co., 1964); Arnold Foster and Benjamin R. Epstein, *Danger on the Right* (New York: Random House, 1964).

    4. *Listen, America!* p. 101.

    5. As described in the book with that name cited earlier, *The Fundamentalist Phenomenon*.

    6. Tom Minnery illustrates the failure to make these distinctions by the cover of *A.D.* magazine, which supplies visual background for a feature article by Roger Shinn ("Moral Majority: Distorting Faith and Patriotism," Vol. 10, No. 6 [June/July, 1981], pp. 15 – 17) with a picture from a Washington rally Falwell did not attend or support, showing participants in "charismatic prayer" arm movements uncharacteristic of Falwell fundamentalists. Minnery is correct about the shortcomings of the press coverage—religious as well as secular— of the Moral Majority. However, it should be noted that in the same paragraph he mistakenly refers to "the United Presbyterian magazine *A.D.*" *A.D.* is a joint publication of the United Presbyterian Church, U.S.A. and the United Church of Christ, and Roger Shinn is a well-known United Church of Christ theologian. There are two separate editions of each issue, making such misidentification as understandable in our less-than-ecumenical age as similar confusions in mainline Christianity about the Religious Right.

    7. A term used by Richard Viguerie to describe the coalitions of the New Right.

    8. Martin Marty's term for the "zone" occupied by "mainline Protestant,

evangelical and Catholic" constituencies that take responsibility for the public arena, demonstrated in the '60s by their leadership in civil rights and peace movements. For an examination of Falwell's switch from a quietist to an activist position vis à vis church involvement in civil affairs, see Frances FitzGerald, "A Disciplined, Charging Army," *The New Yorker,* May 18, 1981, pp. 60 – 63, 113 – 114.

9. See Gabriel Fackre, *The Christian Story: A Narrative Interpretation of Christian Doctrine* (Grand Rapids: William B. Eerdmans Publishing Co., 1978).

10. Thus Moral Majoritian Tim LaHaye is right in his statement, "Simply defined humanism is man's attempt to solve his problems independently of God [sic]," *The Battle for the Mind* (Old Tappan, N.J.: Fleming H. Revell Company, 1980), p. 26. However, he goes on to import into his definition of what does and does not constitute human megalomania: a) a series of partisan human opinions on economics, politics, art, science, and education; b) limitation of anthropocentrism to the atheist and thus an excision of the biblical judgment on the human self-assertion of the religious; c) a too quick accession to the secular definition of secular humanism made by those who have instutionalized their form of it in Ethical Culture Societies and Manifestos; and d) a confusion of the natural theology tradition of Aquinas and his successors (who most certainly did not raise "human wisdom to a level equal with biblical revelation," p. 29) and the stream of western Christian humanism with his simpler definition and his inflated definition that includes "atheism, evolution, amorality, autonomous man and a socialist — one world view" (pp. 57 – 96). These mistaken historical and theological judgments are traceable, in part, to the conception of revelation behind this statement: "The wisdom of man, often called secular humanism today, can be traced back to the rudimentary writings of man. In fact, only two lines of reasoning permeate all literature: biblical revelation and the wisdom of man. All books are based on either man's thoughts or God's thoughts" (*ibid.,* p. 27). This view diverges from Protestant orthodoxy which LaHaye claims to represent. Conservative Protestantism acknowledges the role in God's plan of "general revelation" (Rom. 1:19 – 20), and thus extra-biblical sources in nature, history, and conscience for moral and spiritual perception (helpful albeit not salvific because of the damaged image of God in us, therefore requiring "special revelation").

CHAPTER 1

1. "The Moral Majority is not a Christian organization. . . . We are made up of fundamentalists, evangelicals, Roman Catholics, conservative Jews, Mormons and even persons of no religious belief who share our concerns about the issues we address." Falwell, "The Maligned Moral Majority," *Newsweek,* p. 17.

2. For origins and linkages of New Right — Religious Right figures and movements see Richard Viguerie, *The New Right: We're Ready to Lead* (Falls Church, Va: The Viguerie Company, 1980), pp. 39 – 102. Also note Falwell's introduction to this book and the sixteen pages of photographs showing interlocking movements and leadership. See also Jorstad, *The Politics of Moralism,* pp. 73 – 75 on "Assembling the Moral Majority"; FitzGerald, *The New Yorker,* pp. 124 – 126; Hadden and Swann, *Prime Time Preachers,* pp. 135 – 144.

3. FitzGerald, *The New Yorker,* pp. 53 – 141. Hadden and Swann question Falwell's membership figures for Moral Majority. The "four million" figure, cited in the pamphlet "Moral Majority Celebrates its Second Birthday!", is up

from the earlier two and three million to which Hadden and Swann refer;
"During the campaign Falwell variously claimed 2 to 3 million members for
Moral Majority, including 72,000 pastors. The numbers just don't square with
the evidence. For one thing, Moral Majority doesn't really have a national
membership. In October 1980 Michael Farris, executive director of Moral Majority of Washington State, claimed that his membership of 12,000 was the
largest of the fifty state chapters. By simple arithmetic, if every state had that
many members, Moral Majority would be 600,000 strong not 2 to 3 million.
By Falwell's own admission, the circulation of the *Moral Majority Report* at
election time was 482,000. If Moral Majority itself had 2 to 3 million members,
are we to believe that only one-fourth to one-sixth received the organization's
newspaper?" (*Prime Time Preachers*, pp. 164 – 165).

4. The size of Falwell's television audience and that of the "electronic
preachers" in general is much in dispute. For details consult William Martin,
"The Birth of a Media Myth," *The Atlantic*, Vol. 247, No. 6 (June 1981), pp. 7 – 16.
See also James Franklin, "The Religious Right: Its Political Clout Overstated,"
The Boston Globe Focus (July 19, 1981), pp. A1, A4. The Neilsen survey esti-
mates an audience for Falwell's "Old-Time Gospel Hour" at 1,440,000 with
a 2.3 drop from February 1980 to December 1980. The overall audience of the
"prime-time preachers" is estimated to be 13,767,000. The figures from this
survey contrast sharply with Ben Armstrong's estimate in *The Electric Church*
(Nashville: Thomas Nelson Publishers, 1979), p. 7, of 130 million people watch-
ing television and listening to the radio on a Sunday morning.

5. To which must be added his subsequent "Agenda for the Eighties"
chapter in *The Fundamentalist Phenomenon*. Both of these documents are
the environing philosophy and goals of the "moral majority," but are to be
distinguished technically from the more limited purposes of Moral Majority,
Inc., as previously noted.

In discussing both upper and lower case "Moral Majority," the comments
from two issues of the Moral Majority Report are interesting. A short article
entitled "54% of all Americans Consider Themselves Members of the Moral
Majority" cites a *People* magazine's May 18 survey in which its pollsters asked:
"Do you consider yourself a member of the Moral Majority?" According to the
magazine, "Most—54 percent—feel they belong to at least a lower-case moral
majority . . . " (*ibid.*, p. 5). A somewhat different view is expressed in the April 20,
1981 issue in "Ask the Editor?????": "Unfortunately, many journalists now use
the term 'moral majority' (Small ms) as a catch-all for anything in the new
religious right. That means that we get connected with many issues that we
are not associated with" (*ibid*, p. 14).

6. A major difference of opinion has to do with "the gift of tongues," as
Falwell rejects the charismatic views and practice of Robertson, Bakker, and
Robison. See "Doctrinal Position on Tongues Movement," Office of Admissions,
Liberty Baptist College.

7. Robert Sandon, "Religious Piety and Political Reaction." Public Policy
Conference at LaForest, Colorado (Board for Homeland Ministries, United
Church of Christ), p. 609.

8. For a careful listing of the "anti" and "pro" platforms of the New
Right – Religious Right see Jorstad, *The Politics of Moralism*, pp. 76 – 78. For
the personnel and programs of the New Right see Viguerie, *The New Right:
We're Ready to Lead*, pp. 15 – 17 and *passim*. For a listing of New Right groups
with special reference to their funding from Scaife resources see *Common
Cause*, August 1981, pp. 13 – 15.

9. Viguerie, *The New Right*, pp. 8, 48, 152, 225. Schwarz's views are developed in *You Can Trust the Communists (to be Communists)* (Englewood Cliffs, N.J.: Prentice-Hall, Inc., 1960). Forster and Epstein identify him as a leader of the Radical Right and devote twenty pages to a study of his views and movement; see *Danger on the Right*, pp. 47 – 67.

10. "*Penthouse* Interview: Reverend Jerry Falwell," *Penthouse*, March 1981, pp. 150 – 151. This "secular humanist" publication which secured an interview with Falwell without his knowledge of its ultimate print location appropriately displayed the stigmata of its world view by its reference to Falwell's belief in "biblical inherency" (p. 151). Falwell responded to the *Penthouse* maneuver to acquire the interview by an "Emergency!" appeal for funds with "I Did Not Give An Interview To *Penthouse* Magazine" on the envelope and letterhead of a Moral Majority mailing (Feb. 9, 1981).

11. The "creationist" campaign to alter science teaching in the public schools is not a major plank in the platform of the political New Right. For another interesting deviation from the general New Right program note Viguerie's opposition to capital punishment (*The New Right*, pp. 215 – 216).

12. Ellul's discussion of humanism and its six principles in his book *The New Demons* is cited in Glenn E. Fox, *Encyclopedia for Christian Schools* (Dallas: Life, Inc., 1980), p. 506.

13. "The free enterprise system is clearly outlined in the Book of Proverbs in the Bible" (Falwell, *Listen, America!*, p. 12). One of Falwell's most quoted authorities on this and related matters is Robert Ringer, author of *Restoring the American Dream* (New York: QED/Harper & Row, 1979). Ringer is also the author of *Looking Out for Number 1* and *Winning Through Intimidation* and other works which espouse a "selfist" philosophy.

14. Quoted by FitzGerald, *The New Yorker*, p. 135. Falwell makes frequent use of military metaphors: "The local church is an organized army equipped for battle, ready to charge the enemy. . . . The Sunday school is the attacking squad. . . . The Church should be a disciplined, charging army. . . . Christians, like slaves and soldiers, ask no questions. . . . Radio became the artillery that broke up my fallow ground and set me to thinking and searching, but the local church became the occupation force that finished the job and completed the task the artillery had begun. It is important to bombard our territory, to move out near the coast and shell the enemy. . . . But ultimately some Marines have to march in, encounter the enemy face-to-face, and put the flag up, that is, build the local church. . . . I am speaking to Marines who have been called of God to move in past the shelling, the bombing and the foxholes and, with bayonet in hand, encounter the enemy face-to-face and one-on-one bring them under submission to the Gospel of Christ . . . " (sermon and statements quoted by FitzGerald, pp. 107, 108). The battle imagery is pervasive in the writing and speaking of the Religious Right. "We are in a battle—and it takes armies to win wars" (LaHaye, *The Battle for the Mind*, p. 225).

15. Quoted by FitzGerald, *The New Yorker*, p. 116.

CHAPTER 2

1. See George H. Williams, *The Radical Reformation* (Philadelphia: Westminster Press, 1962), *passim*.

2. Sydney Ahlstrom, *A Religious History of the American People* (New

Haven: Yale University Press, 1972), pp. 124 – 150, 555 – 568, 805 – 824, 842 – 856, 909 – 915.

3. On the influence of Zoroastrianism on the early Christian teacher Bardaisan, see Steven Runciman, *The Medieval Manichee: A Study of the Christian Dualist Heresy* (Cambridge: The University Press, 1947), pp. 11 – 12, 27. This book is an indispensible resource for understanding "the Christian Dualist Heresy," especially as it was influenced by Mani. See also Augustine, *The Catholic and Manichaean Ways of Life*, trans. by Donald A. Gallagher and Idella J. Gallagher in *The Fathers of The Church*, Vol. 56 (Washington, D.C.: The Catholic University of America Press, 1966).

4. This analysis appears in my section of *Youth Ministry* by Jan Chartier and Gabriel Fackre (Philadelphia: Judson Press, 1979), pp. 11 – 23. Pages 14 to 23 of this book are excerpted here in a somewhat revised form.

5. See FitzGerald, *The New Yorker*, pp. 60 – 62.

6. *Ibid.* pp. 120 – 122.

7. On the organization of Donald Wildmon's "Coalition for Better Television" and a fall 1980 report of the results of the television monitoring program of the National Federation for Decency (percentage ratios for specific programs on "Sex incidents per hour," "Top sponsors of profanity," etc.) see *NFD Informer*, February 1981.

8. Cited by FitzGerald in *The New Yorker*, p. 63.

CHAPTER 3

1. *The Christian Story*, pp. 20 – 51.

2. "The basic tenet of former *evangelical* Christianity, now what I call *fundamentalist* Christianity, is that we have one basic document on which we predicate everything we believe, our faith, our practice, our life-style, our homes, et cetera, government—is the inherency [sic] of scripture, not only in matters of theology, but science, geography, history et cetera—totally and entirely, the very word of God" (Falwell interview, *Penthouse*, p. 151).

3. In addition to LaHaye's *Battle of the Mind* cited earlier, see "Secular Humanism: What It Is!", *Moral Majority Report*, May 18, 1981, p. 3, for a characterization of the phenomenon. The Christian Broadcasting Network's "Let their Eyes be Opened" is a thirty-minute film that seeks to show the influence of secular humanism in the public schools. For an account of the campaign against secular humanism see "The Right's New Bogeyman," *Newsweek*, July 6, 1981, pp. 48 – 50 and *The New York Times*, "Parents Groups Purging Schools of Humanist Books and Classes," May 17, 1981, pp. 1, 52.

CHAPTER 4

1. "Creationism" is methodically set forth in the curriculum produced for Christian Academies by Accelerated Christian Education, Inc. For a description of the nature and influence of this curriculum see "The Genesis of a Program Built on Creation," in "Spring Survey of Education," *The New York Times*, April 26, 1981, pp. 18 – 19. For the mounting resistance to this movement see Isaac Asimov, "The Threat of Creationism," *The New York Times Magazine*, June 14, 1981, pp. 90 – 101. The theological carelessness of Asimov's argument at certain critical points provides the Religious Right with

evidence for its contention that its critics do not understand it or the issues at stake. Asimov confuses the specific argument from design of ancient vintage and the general faith assertion of the existence of a Creator, both of which are incorporated in creationist literature, with the essential point of the creationist argument—that the specifics of the cosmology in Genesis 1 and 2 are an alternative reading of scientific history and therefore have a legitimate place in science books alongside the evolutionary hypothesis. By clumsily merging these two matters Asimov places by implication all theists (including Teilhard de Chardin) in the creationist category. The conventional wisdom of "secular humanism" may indeed place all theists in a common camp, but this philosophical judgment obscures the controverted question of "creationism" in the schools.

An astute observation on issues at stake is made by Robert Root-Bernstein of the Salk Institute.

Theories must not only be predictive (or postdictive) and falsifiable; they must also limit what data are possible a priori. Evolutionism is a theory according to these criteria. It could be falsified by evidence that its predictions indicate should not exist. Yet, in more than 100 years of research, no such data have been discovered. Thus, the validity of the theory has been established by its historical record. It is this historical record of research, in turn, that gives the theory its important epistemological status in science.

Theories must do even more than predict or limit, however; they must also provide criteria for the evaluation of data. As any scientist knows, not all observed data are valid. Some can be interpreted as factual (that is, they fit the theory); some are artifactual (that is, the result of secondary or accidental influences not covered by the theory); and some are anomalies (that is, demonstrably not due to secondary influences, but also at odds with predictions from theory). Evolutionism provides such criteria for data evaluation. A perfect example is the case of Piltdown "man." Evolutionary theory predicted a "missing link" between the apes and man. Piltdown "man" was thought at first to be that desired link until it was demonstrated to be an artifact (due to human conniving) because it did not meet the anatomical criteria predicted for the missing link according to theory. Thus, while evolutionary theory calls for a "missing link"—or more accurately, a series of such links—it also specifies the criteria by which any suspected link may be evaluated as factual, artifactual, or anomalous. In short, a theory must incorporate means for self-correction. Evolutionary explanations qualify as theories on these grounds.

But whether evolutionary theory is valid or not is only half the question in the present debates. For some reason most scientists are so busy defending their own discipline that they fail to see that the crux of the matter lies in the creationist camp. Can creationist accounts of life qualify as scientific theories? No—on no account. They are neither predictive nor postdictive. They do not limit what is possible in history; or, if they do (as in stating the age of the earth), they fail to do so in verifiable or falsifiable ways. Neither do they set criteria for the evaluation of data as fact, artifact, or anomaly. These creationist explanations have not even accrued epistemological validity through a history of accummulated research. ("Letters," *Science*, Vol. 212 [June 26, 1981], pp. 1446 — 1448.)

After making this eminently reasonable case, Root-Bernstein weakens his argument with the broadside, "And worst of all, creationist accounts are au-

113

thoritarian, based primarily upon revelation rather than reason. Creationism is therefore not science; it is dogma" (p. 1448). The sharp juxstaposition of "revelation" and "reason" is an old Enlightenment orthodoxy which does not take into account the function of mystery and imagination in scientific discovery and method. On this matter see Harold Schilling, *The New Consciousness in Science and Religion* (Philadelphia: United Church Press, 1973).

2. One of them is Falwell: "If you'll read the first three chapters of Genesis carefully, there's a very clear, unlimited time span there. It could have been millions of years; it could have been hundreds of millions of years" (*Penthouse*, p. 151).

3. For the progress of political efforts to incorporate the creationist view in public school textbooks see *Science and Government Report*, June 15, 1981.

4. Opening sentences of the Apostles' Creed and the Nicene Creed.

5. For an overview of the man and his philosophy see the *Newsweek* cover story, June 29, 1981, pp. 22 – 32. His widely quoted apocalyptic cum environment remark is, "I don't know how many future generations we can count on before the Lord returns" (p. 29).

6. For an elaboration of these themes see my "Ecology and Theology," in Ian Barbour, ed., *Western Man and Environmental Ethics* (Reading, Mass.: Addison-Wesley Publishing Co., 1973).

7. For an exploration of inclusive motifs in Scripture long obscured by patriarchal interpretations see Phyllis Tribble, *God and the Rhetoric of Sexuality* (Philadelphia: Fortress Press, 1978).

8. For example, Paul K. Jewett, *The Ordination of Women: An Essay on the Office of Christian Ministry* (Grand Rapids: William B. Eerdmans Publishing Co., 1980).

9. Reinhold Niebuhr, *The Nature and Destiny of Man*, Vol. 1 (New York: Charles Scribner's Sons, 1941), *passim*.

10. For example, Mark 10:21 – 24 (Matt. 19:21 – 24, Luke 18:22 – 25); Luke 1:53; 6:24; 16:19 – 31.

11. Considering the attack of the Religious Right on evolutionary theory it is startling to find a concurrence of views on one of the most suspect aspects of the latter: the doctrine of "the survival of the fittest." This doctrine found its way from early evolutionary speculation into the dogma of late nineteenth-century capitalism. Industrial barons were only too happy to use Darwinian data on the survival of some species that seemed to legitimate fierce struggle for limited resources, the rise to power of the strong, and the elimination of the weak in "dog-eat-dog" competition. There is no blatant endorsement of this economic Darwinianism in the explicit teaching of the Religious Right—how could there be with its "creationist" rejection of "evolutionism"?—but the pronouncements that competition is "biblical" (Falwell, *Listen America!*, p. 12) and that the free enterprise system and the work ethic are the plan of Jesus Christ share some basic assumptions about the survival of the fittest and the consequent just deserts that come to those who fall by the wayside.

The esteem in which the strong and successful are held, not only in the economic arena but also in political, military, familial, and ecclesiastical life also indicates the convergence of Religious Right teaching with the survival of the fittest theme in evolutionary theory. We shall explore this presently in the "mighty man" philosophy.

For all the protestations about secular humanism's evolutionary standpoint, we find evident in the working doctrine of the Religious Right one of the former's morally suspect derivatives. Here is an irony we shall regularly confront: secular humanism making its backdoor entrance into the sanctuaries of modern piety.

CHAPTER 5

1. The juxtaposition is a refrain in the appeals of Moral Majority, Inc. Falwell writes in a letter to supporters, May 6, 1981: "Right now at this very moment, liberals and pornography kings are banding together to destroy us. . . . To make sure that good and moral Americans know the truth about what is going on in Washington and across this nation—and how Moral Majority is working to bring this nation back to moral sanity."

In endorsing Viguerie's book on the New Right, Falwell says in the Introduction, "In the last several years, Americans have literally stood by and watched as godless, spineless leaders have brought our nation floundering to the brink of death. . . . The godless minority of treacherous individuals who have been allowed to formulate national policy must now realize they do not represent the majority. They must be made to see that moral Americans are a powerful group who will no longer permit them to destroy our country with their godless, liberal philosophies" (in Viguerie, *The New Right: We're Ready to Lead*, Introduction).

2. "You will find that when society begins to fall apart spiritually, what we find is missing is the mighty man, that man who is willing, with courage and confidence, to stand up for what is right. We are hard-pressed to find today that man in governmental position, that man of war, that judge, that prophet, that preacher who is willing to call sin by its right name" (Falwell, *Listen, America!*, p. 14). The application blank of Moral Majority, Inc., echoes this note: "Recognizing the impending crisis, one man—a man of proven leadership and true vision—has stepped forward. He is Dr. Jerry Falwell, pastor of the Thomas Road Baptist Church in Virginia; preacher on the Old-Time Gospel Hour television program; Chancellor of Liberty Baptist College" (*The Moral Majority, Inc.: Fighting for a Moral America in this Decade of Destiny*).

For another view of the "mighty man" see the second and third chapters of Isaiah. "For the Lord of hosts has a day against all that is lifted up and high. . . . And the haughtiness of man shall be humbled, and the pride of man shall be brought low and the Lord alone will be exalted on that day . . . . For behold, the Lord, the Lord of hosts, is taking away from Jerusalem and from Judah, stay and staff . . . the mighty man and the soldier, the judge and the prophet, the diviner and the elder, the captain of fifty and the man of rank, the counselor and the skillful magician and the expert in charms" (Isa. 2:12, 17; 3:1 – 2).

On the same subject, with special reference to the relation of preacher and prophet to oligarch, see Reinhold Niebuhr, "The Wise Men and the Mighty Men," *Reflections on the End of an Era* (New York: Charles Scribner's Sons, 1934), pp. 39 – 48.

3. On both political realism and naïveté in the democratic tradition see Reinhold Niebuhr, *The Children of Light and the Children of Darkness* (New York: Charles Scribner's Sons, 1944), *passim*.

4. Dualism and the thought patterns of Zoroastrianism are interpreted lucidly by Mary Boyce, *Zoroastrians: Their Religious Beliefs and Practices* (London: Routledge & Kegan Paul, 1979).

5. On this point see Runciman, *The Medieval Manichee*. F. C. Burkitt has produced a helpful overview of Manichean thought and practice: *The Religion of the Manichees* (Cambridge: University Press, 1925; reprinted by AMS Press, 1978).

6. Falwell, *Listen, America!*, p. 12.

7. "Someone often asks—can morality be legislated? The answer is yes. All civilized societies are governed by the legislation of morality—based upon a code of ethics agreed upon by consensus" (Jerry Falwell, "America Was Built on Seven Great Principles," *Moral Majority Report*, May 18, 1981, p. 8).

8. *The Blue Book of the John Birch Society* (Eleventh printing, 1961), p. 138. *Blue Book* proposals two to five for resisting "the conspiracy" are: wider circulation of publications, increasing radio and television influence, coordinated use of "the powerful letter-writing weapon," and the organizing of *ad hoc* committees (pp. 79 – 94). Whereas the soft Radical Right never implemented these plans effectively, the New Right – Religious Right have succeeded with a higher technology and better organizational expertise in a telling way.

9. On scriptural teaching about the rich and the poor see James Wallis, *The Call to Conversion: Recovering the Gospel for These Times* (San Francisco: Harper & Row, 1981), pp. 57ff.

CHAPTER 6

1. "Psalm 9:17 admonishes, 'The wicked shall be turned into hell, and all the nations that forget God.' America is no exception if she forgets God, she too will face his wrath and judgment like every other nation in the history of humanity" (Falwell, *Listen, America!*, p. 21).

On the role of moral law in government: "The Law of Moses and the Law of Christ make up the very heart of the system of laws in the United States of America. If you censor out of the law books of this nation every statute and ethic found in the Old Testament and New Testament, you have nothing but a shambles left" ("America Was Built on Seven Great Principles," *Moral Majority Report*, p. 8).

2. See the chapter "That Miracle Called Israel" in *Listen, America!*, pp. 93 – 98.

3. "Prophecy began to be fulfilled when quite suddenly the Jewish people started immigrating back to their homeland. . . . There is no way that the tiny nation of Israel could have stood against the Arabs in a miraculous six-day war had it not been for the intervention of God Almighty. . . . The last book of the Bible, the Book of Revelation contains prophecy regarding future events. Israel plays a significant role in that prophecy . . . " (*ibid.*, pp. 95, 97).

4. On the chosen status and role of the United States see "Freedom's Heritage" in *Listen, America!*, pp. 25 – 43. In addition to the political witness of the nation, America has a special place in God's plan of evangelism: "Our freedoms are essential to world evangelism in this latter part of the twentieth century" (p. 214).

5. Falwell, *Listen, America!*, pp. 215 – 223 and numerous Moral Majority mailings.

6. As in the attack on Falwell by James Combs, "Racial Hatred" and "Faith and Fate," in *Christian Vanguard: Official Publication of the New Christian Crusade Church*, April 1981, pp. 3 – 4, 13 – 14.

7. Donald Dayton observes, "Concern over homosexuality . . . permeates the group's literature; yet the Bible speaks directly to this issue in only a handful of texts, several of which are obscure and difficult. But there are literally hundreds of biblical texts that speak of justice and of God's concern for the poor. Faith that does not grasp the pervasiveness of this theme in Scripture is not biblical faith. This concern, however, is not cultivated in the Moral Majority literature I have examined; indeed, it is contradicted. Obviously some other (cultural?) filter is at work in this reading of 'biblical morality'" ("Distinguishing Good Religion from Bad," in "What's Wrong with Born-Again Politics?", *The Christian Century*, p. 1003).

8. "The Jews are returning to their land of unbelief. They are spiritually blind and desperately in need of their Messiah and Savior. Yet they are God's people, and in the world today Bible-believing Christians in America are the best friends the nation Israel has" (Falwell, *Listen, America!*, p. 98). The details of how Israel will fare in the apocalyptic scenario of the Religious Right (Chapter 10) should be of interest to Jews today who court the pro-Israel constituencies of the Religious Right. Further, the sin-suffering theodicy set forth on pp. 93 – 96 of *Listen, America!* merits careful reflection.

9. "A few of you here today don't like Jews. And I know why. He can make more money accidentally than you can on purpose" (Falwell on the steps of the Virginia state capitol, as quoted by FitzGerald, *The New Yorker*, p. 115). On pp. 114 – 116 FitzGerald discusses the evidences of stereotyping within Falwell organizations.

10. In speaking about the "evangelical nationalists" James Wallis says that "the problem is not that they mix faith and politics; biblical faith has a political meaning. The problem is this patriotic religion does not stand for the same things as the original evangel. . . . The evangelical nationalists perpetuate a theology of empire" (Wallis, *Call to Conversion*, p. 26).

CHAPTER 7

1. The themes of the Definition of Chalcedon, 451. See John Leith, ed., *Creeds of the Churches* (Garden City: Doubleday & Co., 1963), pp. 34 – 36, and Fackre, *The Christian Story*, pp. 89 – 111.

2. On the relation of the doctrine of the incarnation to political involvement see George Macleod, *We Shall Rebuild* (Glasgow: Iona Community, n.d.). "It is the personal challenge to anyone who truly grasps the meaning of the Incarnation—that God became man, that he clothed Himself in the physical and thereby declared holiness to be inseparable from 'material' considerations" (p. 18).

3. *The Myth of God Incarnate* is representative of a flurry of current christological reconsiderations that call into question the classical affirmations about the deity and singularity of Christ.

4. A passage from Archibald Hodge's work on the atonement sheds light on the view of the Religious Right. Fairly criticizing the conception of atonement that dissolves "justice" into "benevolence" he goes on to say, however: "We agree that benevolence respects the happiness of others, and that benevolence is a moral excellence which ornaments the divine nature and which men *ought* to possess and to exercise. But the idea of oughtness is more elemental than the idea of benevolence, and it cannot be analyzed into anything more elemental. It is an independent and ultimate idea which stands

by itself. But *if* the idea of moral obligation is ultimate and independent, it follows from its very nature, that it is intrinsically supreme and absolute. Its dictates may coincide with those of benevolence, but if not, they *must* take precedence of them" (*The Atonement* [Philadelphia: Presbyterian Board of Publications, 1867], p. 26). A Kantian philosophical premise here exercises such inordinate influence on the formulation of a Christian doctrine that the far more subtle dialectic of justice and benevolence in the divine nature is obscured, and the understanding of the atonement is, in turn, adversely affected.

5. H. Richard Niebuhr, *The Kingdom of God in America* (New York: Harper and Brothers, 1959), p. 193.

6. Robert Paul's observation in *The Atonement and the Sacraments* (New York: Abingdon Press, 1960).

7. For an exploration of this theme see *The Christian Story*, pp. 117 – 121, 133 – 138, and for its detailed exposition see my forthcoming systematics volume on the atonement.

8. Falwell illustrates the controlling influence of secular right premises in a revealing response to an interviewer's question in *Christianity Today* about Moral Majority, Inc.'s campaign against drugs. Question: "Do you put alcohol, and tobacco under drugs?" Answer: "Yes, we do with alcohol, but not tobacco. We have lots of Moral Majority members who smoke. People say, Why don't you guys get more involved in this? Or someone will say, What about the poor? We could never bring the issue of the poor into Moral Majority because the argument would be, Who is going to decide what we teach those people? Mormons, Catholics? No, we won't get into that. As private persons and ministers, we make a commitment if we feel convicted. But for Moral Majority, no! If we go in there, create jobs, raise funds, and get involved with the local pastors, the problem is, which pastors? If we say the Mormon pastors, the Fundamentalists are gone. If we say the Catholic pastors, the Jews are gone, and so forth. We just have to stay away from helping the poor" ("An Interview with the Lone Ranger of American Fundamentalism," *Christianity Today*, p. 27).

Two points come clear in this assertation: (1) What defines "moral" for those pastors and church members who express their Christian moral witness in this political organization is the agenda of the right-wing political movement and not the biblical charter in which ministry to and with the poor is at the very center of prophetic-apostolic moral teaching and an eschatological test of faithfulness to Jesus Christ (Matt. 25:31 – 46). The smoking habits of some adherents—and no doubt also the tobacco interests for which Moral Majority supporter Jesse Helms seeks government supports—determine the moral agenda of an organization whose "most agressive leaders . . . are fundamentalist pastors" (*ibid*, p. 23). On this matter also a secular right political platform determines the posture of the Religious Right. For an account of the piety and politics of Senator Helms see *Time* cover story "To the Right, March!", September 14, 1981, pp. 24 – 39.

9. For a powerful statement of the biblical mandates on justice for the poor see evangelical Waldron Scott's *Bring Forth Justice* (Grand Rapids: William B. Eerdmans Publishing Co., 1980).

10. John Milton, "On the Morning of Christ's Nativity."

CHAPTER 8

1. *The Christian Story,* pp. 147 – 151.

2. "My definition of a fundamentalist is one who, first, believes in the inerrancy of Scripture, and second, is committed to biblical separation in the world and to the Lordship of Christ. For me, the definition of separation from the world may be different from some others'. I don't use alcoholic beverages and I preach teetotalism. That would be the practice of 18,000 members of this church. I don't think it has anything to do with salvation. But when I talk about separation, I mean separation from the rock music culture, separation from immorality, separation from the Hollywood culture" (Falwell interview, *Christianity Today,* p. 23).

3. FitzGerald, *The New Yorker,* p. 73.

4. On "God's chain of command" in church and family see *ibid.,* pp. 96, 74.

5. Donald Michael's phrase in "Twenty-first Century Institutions: Prerequisites for a Creative and Responsible Society," *Human Values and Advancing Technology,* compiled by Cameron P. Hall (New York: Friendship Press, 1967), pp. 103 – 104.

6. Independent churches may hold membership in a "fellowship" of like-minded congregations such as the Baptist Bible Fellowship which numbers 3500 churches including the Thomas Road Baptist Church. See *The Fundamentalist Phenomenon,* pp. 126 – 128. These loosely knit associations do not function as communities of accountability and support as is the case in most denominations, national churches, or world communions.

7. The determined effort of Religious Right preachers like Falwell to maintain the church/state separation and avoid both theological and tax problems is not germane here. We must believe Falwell when he says he faithfully separates the programs of the Moral Majority, Inc., from those of the Thomas Road Baptist Church. ("Moral Majority for me is definitely a movement in which I am involved as a private citizen—period! I do not involve Thomas Road Baptist Church. The church has never given a dollar to the movement. When our people come here to church they hear the Bible taught and preached, they don't hear Moral Majority. I doubt if I've mentioned the words Moral Majority 10 times in Thomas Road Baptist Church" (Falwell interview, *Christianity Today,* p. 23).

The point being made in the text is that partisan political allegiance is not limited either to endorsing candidates and parties or supporting political institutions like Moral Majority, Inc. It can be powerfully operative in the very midst of occasions when "the Bible [is] taught and preached." This takes place when preached and taught moral judgments either exactly replicate current political opinion (a detailed "pro-family" view that corresponds item for item with a pro-family congressional bill) or are explicitly expressed in positions taken in the pulpit or congregation as in the anti-ERA campaigns of the Religious Right.

8. For example, the general mandates on peace, justice, freedom, and respect for the environment, and the middle axioms that relate these to the poor, the hungry, the minorities, Third World countries, women, elders, and the disabled, and to ecological and energy imperatives.

9. The current effort to recover the ministry of the whole people of God is chronicled in *Laity Exchange* (edited by Mark Gibbs), discussed in a variety

119

of essays in *Theology Today,* Vol. XXXVI, No. 3 (October 1979), and tested in congregational laboratories in the Laity Project led by Richard Boholm at Andover Newton Theological School.

10. On the "mighty [church] man" note Falwell's sermon, "The Day of Great Men Has Not Passed." He says, "God's plan is that His flock is to be led by shepherds, not run by a board or a committee. . . . God never intended for a committee nor a board of deacons nor any other group to dominate a church or control a pastor. The pastor is God's man, God's servant, God's leader. When you tie the hands of God's man, when you keep him from acting as the Holy Spirit leads him, you have murdered his initiative, you have killed his spirit." Quoted in FitzGerald, *The New Yorker,* p. 96.

On Falwell's view of "democracy": "Today we find that America is more of a democracy than a republic. Sometimes there is mob rule. In some instances a vocal minority prevails. Our Founding Fathers would not accept the tyranny of a democracy because they recognized that the only sovereign over men and nations was Almighty God. A republic is a government of law. In a republic there are checks and balances, and the majority represent the individual" (*Listen, America!,* p. 44).

11. FitzGerald quotes "a professor who worked with the Moral Majority" as saying, "Imagine a spectrum that runs from a Jim Jones cult on the one hand to the most arid of liberal churches on the other. . . . Well, some of the big fundamentalist churches in the South would fall close—dangerously close—to the Jim Jones end of the spectrum. I know because I used to belong to one of them. I got out, but it was a terrible culture shock" (*The New Yorker,* p. 96). The professor continues, "The question is, of course, where Dr. Falwell's church would fit in this spectrum. It is one of the religious kingdoms of the South. But in my view it is one of the most liberal and progressive of them" (*ibid.*).

CHAPTER 9

1. "I'm a Bible-believing, Christ-exalting, soul-winning preacher" (Falwell interview, *Christianity Today,* p. 24); "Each and every man and woman alive today needs a new birth experience" (Falwell, *Listen, America!,* p. 54).

2. "America is desperately in need of divine healing, which can only come if God's people will humble themselves, pray, seek His face and turn from their wicked ways. . . . We have become one of the most blatantly sinful nations of all time. . . . The time for national repentance of God's people has now come to America" (*Listen, America!,* pp. 213, 217).

3. *The Christian Story,* pp. 190–194.

4. For an examination of the four "turning points" in Christian conversion see my *Word in Deed* (Grand Rapids: William B. Eerdmans Publishing Co., 1975), pp. 79–98.

5. But what are the messages of the electronic churches? Here too they have imitated the success formulas of commercial television. Most religious television, like its secular counterpart, deals largely in simple solutions to human problems. Television can't handle complicated material very well. Unless one can afford the luxury of time and money for imaginative illustration, one is limited to what can be *said.* And what is said must be said quickly and extremely simply, or the audience won't understand. Furthermore, audiences also want

to be entertained. And they want to be made to feel good. When they are made to feel bad, they turn to another channel. . . .

Most TV preachers have gone beyond saying that it is all right to think about yourself. Get right with God, they say, and you won't have to wait until the next life for your rewards. . . .

The manner in which the televangelists sell their message must conform to the logic of television, whose stock-in-trade is an endless stream of easy answers to difficult questions. The most difficult human problems are brought to satisfactory resolution in one hour. Many require only a half hour. Many more are handled in just thirty seconds, the length of most television commercials. (Hadden and Swann, *Prime-Time Preachers*, pp. 12 – 13, 100.)

6. For "The business of TV religion" see Hadden and Swann, *Prime Time Preachers*, pp. 103 – 124.

CHAPTER 10

1. For observations on this relationship see the thesis of Robert Jewett, *The Captain America Complex: The Dilemma of Zealous Nationalism* (Philadelphia: Westminster Press, 1973), pp. 116ff. Paul D. Hanson is less impressed with the Persian influence, arguing that "apocalyptic eschatology" rises out of Jewish roots and in particular the dimmed hopes of early visionaries for historical fulfilments (*The Dawn of Apocalypse* [Philadelphia: Fortress Press, 1975]).

2. Quoted in FitzGerald, *The New Yorker*, p. 60.

3. *The Christian Story*, pp. 206 – 229.

4. For details see Charles Taylor, *The Destiny Chart: Today in Bible Prophecy*, 1978. Falwell developed his own similar scenarios in six "Old Time Gospel Hour" sermons during the summer of 1980.

For regular commentary on current apocalyptic thinking see *End-Time News Digest*, edited by Jim McKeever, Medford, Oregon. In an issue on "The Tribulation Temple," McKeever writes: "We know that before Christ returns and before the great Tribulation begins, there must be a 'temple'. . . . It may be that this Tribulation temple is already under construction, as the Jerusalem Great Synagogue. If the Jerusalem Great Synagogue is not the Tribulation temple, my best analysis is that it will be some structure that is constructed near, but not on, the temple mount. The Jerusalem Great Synagogue seems to meet all of the requirements for the Tribulation temple because it is designed as the central focal place of Jewish worship for the entire world and even has an Oriental wing for conducting services in Japanese. If the dictator beast were going to make a religious compact with the Jewish religious leaders in the near future, this would be the most likely place for it to occur" (Issue 031 [April 1981], pp. 7 – 8).

5. Werner Elert's characterization. "The dogma aims to formulate the stable element of the kerygma" (Elert, *The Last Things*, trans. by Martin Bertram and ed. by Rudolph F. Nordern [St. Louis: Concordia Publishing House, 1974], p. 8).

CHAPTER 11

1. P. T. Forsyth struggles profoundly with this dialectic in *The Work of Christ* (London: Collins, The Fontana Library, 1965). See also *The Christian Story*, pp. 240 – 243.

CONCLUSION

1. From "The Theological Declaration of Barmen," in Arthur Cochrane, *The Church's Confession Under Hitler* (Philadelphia: Westminster Press, 1962), pp. 237 – 242.

2. Mark O. Hatfield, "Foreward" to *The Fear Brokers* by Senator Thomas J. McIntyre with John C. Obert (New York: The Pilgrim Press, 1979), p. xvi.

3. See earlier discussion on pages 33 – 35.

Index

Index

Index